Manners from Heaven

Quentin Crisp is the author of *The Naked Civil Servant* (available in Flamingo) and *How to Become a Virgin* (available in Fontana). He now lives in New York.

Quentin Crisp
with John Hofsess

Manners from Heaven

A Divine Guide to
Good Behaviour

FLAMINGO

Published by Fontana Paperbacks

First published by Hutchinson & Co. (Publishers) Ltd 1984

This Flamingo edition first published
in 1985 by Fontana Paperbacks,
8 Grafton Street, London W1X 3LA

Phototypeset in Linotron Trump Mediaeval
by Tradespools Ltd, Frome, Somerset
Made and printed in Great Britain
by William Collins Sons & Co. Ltd, Glasgow

To Wayne Brown –
and the next generation

Contents

'My generation of radicals and breakers-down never found anything to take the place of the old virtues of work and courage and the old graces of courtesy and politeness.'

F. Scott Fitzgerald (Letter to his daughter quoted in *F. Scott Fitzgerald, A Biography* by Andre Le Vot)

A Note of Thanks

Many people have made important contributions to the development of this book, some of whom shall remain nameless because their contribution consisted of providing the authors with harrowing examples of bad manners which we would rather forget and which, in a few cases, took weeks to recover from.

The following people are those without whose assistance the book could never have been completed: Edmund White, author of *A Boy's Own Story*; Felicity Mason, author of *The Love Habit*; Kirkpatrick Sale, author of *Human Scale*; Jane Gale, editor of *Homemaker* magazine in Toronto; Canadian critic Clyde Gilmour and his wife, Barbara, whose cheerful comments were always a delight; American film-makers Case Chapman and Bob Alvarez; Guy Pace, Assistant Executive Secretary of Actor's Equity in New York; the staff of the Department of Creative Writing, University of British Columbia.

Special thanks to editor Susan Hill who first suggested the idea, and to literary agent Connie Clausen who indefatigably champions the art of Crisperanto. It is through knowing such people that the authors realize that only insignificant debts can ever be repaid.

Foreword

Nothing more rapidly inclines a person to go into a monastery than reading a book on etiquette. There are so many trivial ways in which it is possible to commit some social sin. This book endeavours to circumnavigate this effect. It tells you neither how to eat an artichoke nor how to address an archbishop. You can avoid both these hazardous experiences and yet enjoy a rich, full life. I am not concerned with pettipoints of etiquette. There are, I know, devotees of dining-table manners who regard discussions about 'whether it is or is not proper to light tapers at a luncheon' as dealing with a burning issue, but I see such matters as trifling. I am more concerned with how manners can be employed to cope with, or outwit, the affronts of racism, sexism, hooliganism – and the terrible things which people do to one another in the name of love.

Etiquette is a noun, foreign and abstract. Literally it names the process of attaching labels to things. Metaphorically it is a way of defining people: it is a means of stratification bestowing upon its victims a spurious group value and depriving them of human worth.

Ethically nothing can justify etiquette but, in England in a time when class structure was as rigid as a punk rocker's hair, it was thought socially useful. Each class then felt that, at all cost to humanity, it must keep at barge-pole distance the group by which it seemed itself most seriously threatened – the one immediately below. Beneath the working class there was only a social void. Consequently there was no direction but upward in which the members of this benighted stratum could aim their scorn. This they did by cultivating a negative etiquette just as binding as any other. On every possible occasion they laboriously expressed contempt for all social graces, consigning them to a rubbish heap where they lay alongside art, culture, and other similar affectations. This self-conscious coarseness still exists today – as the popularity of such movies as *Animal House* and *Porky's*, which consist almost entirely of rude noises, attests. But swinish torpor is out of fashion and nowadays only a certain kind of effete homosexual hankering after the strange fruit of 'rough trade' is likely to romanticize the working class and extol its limitations as Whitmanesque virtues.

The aristocracy traditionally pretended to be buddies with the workers – especially in a rural setting. It was the custom for the lord of the manor to dress at least as shabbily as his hirelings, to lean over a rickety gate with the chief of them and to offer him his tobacco pouch. The two men had in common their knowledge of crops, livestock and the weather. Their 'matiness' was apparent rather than real. It relied on the impossibility of encroachment. The social latitudes inhabited by the figures in this affecting tableau of bonhomie were light years apart. In fact the situation masked an unshakeable assumption of authority on the one hand and deference to it on the other. The master addressed his subordinates by their unembellished surnames and occasionally their first names but only because he was certain that replies would never be couched in terms of equal familiarity.

The class for which the gentry expressed not only disdain but open hatred was the nouveau riche, the uppity class of tomorrow. This aversion was illogical. Aristocracy is merely very old money and, if the sources of ancient wealth are investigated, it often transpires that it springs from plunder, tyranny and extortion, whereas most modern riches are accumulated by a shrewd study of the stock market and tax laws. This does not make the venom spewing from the lips of aristocrats any less lethal: its effect is instantly paralysing. Miss Nancy Mitford's famous list of U and Non-U words was intended as light reading. She could afford to laugh at the absurd and arbitrary distinctions between words which were acceptable to the upper classes and others which were taboo. She was brought up with them and knew them by heart. Most of her readers were not: they winced, and worse, they immediately tried to take a crammer's course in verbal snobbery to pass as better-born than they truly were.

Fortunately the rest of the world, not locked into the British Isles, is moving away from etiquette towards manners. A snob is someone who treats breeding and sophistication as though they were moral worth. Snobbery is dying: etiquette, especially as practised by the English, is a form of *exclusion*, a system designed to make people (particularly those not of one's 'class') feel ill at ease and out of place. Manners, on the other hand, especially as practised by Americans, are a technique of *inclusion*, a way of ensuring that in our company no one will ever be made to feel he is an outcast by reason of his birth, education or occupation. To drink from your fingerbowl may be a breach of etiquette, but if a host, seeing his guest make this mistake, did the same, it would be a sign of good manners. It is only this system of manners, with a humanistic base, that anyone can take seriously nowadays.

It was once said that the only difference between a philosopher and anyone else is that the philosopher *wants* to become conscious about what his philosophy is. It could equally be said that practically everyone has some notion of manners, but very few people have given much thought to the prospect of using manners to improve the quality of their lives by behaving with imaginative courtesy towards others. My colleague, John Hofsess, and I believe that anyone who *thinks* about manners will indeed become more ... mannerly. And not merely in a manner of speaking. If it can be said of this book that it is useless to snobs but beneficial to the rest of man (and woman) kind, then it will indeed justify its existence as a guide to good behaviour in the twilight years of the twentieth century, a period so ominous in certain of its trends that some people believe themselves to be the twilight years of the human race. These are difficult days for politeness, and the future often seems to have nothing in store except even more trying conditions of noise, overcrowding, pollution and stress. All these contribute to an impolite society. It is precisely in trying situations that we need our manners most, so a guide to good manners in a time of apocalypse may be appropriate. The fact that someone may drop The Bomb in the middle of our mad tea party should in no way deter us from serving the best tea and the best conversation in our best manner – for ever. Formality should be maintained from the cradle to the grave – and beyond.

New York, 1984

I

Rude Awakenings

'The development from egoism to consideration for others ... is the foundation of all good manners.'

Harold Nicolson, *Good Behaviour*

I confess: For most of my seventy-five years on this cosmic dustball I have been guilty of bad manners. I was ostentatious in appearance – enough to stop traffic on some occasions and interrupt conversations on others. At one time if you had looked down on streets in the city of London from a high window you would only have seen people dressed in black, brown, dark blue or dark grey. Even women did not wear scarlet coats in the street. If you then spotted a blazing Technicolor rash moving slowly through this austere parade it would either have been a fruit cart – or myself.

Good manners require that we tailor our appearance and behaviour to suit a particular person or occasion – but in my flamboyant prime I would have none of that. I would have dressed the same to meet the Queen at Buckingham Palace (wisely, I was never invited) as I did to meet the queens in a King's Road café. I never adjusted my wicked, wanton self: in an era where many thinking people were 'reds' I was outspokenly *rouge*.

When a young man with bright henna hair and a silky, spangled shirt waltzes into a room today like a vamp of the silent screen, his every gesture a neon scream of effeminacy, what gaudy ghosts I see in the rear-view mirror of my own life! But he is either atrociously ill-mannered or else a rock star. Or both.

Good manners would demand that on no account, even by implication, should I bring to light a subject offensive to other people; by going about with my eyelashes blacked, eyebrows plucked, and hair obviously dyed I was dragging into people's consciousness and conversation some sexual reference to myself – about which I would have kept quiet if I had been well mannered.

Most people who take up an attitude expressing an individuality that is far removed from the characteristics of the majority, pass from statement ('I am different . . .') to defiance ('. . . and proud of it!') and then, having gone too far, must move back to the middle. I no longer cast about for weirder, wilder things to say or wear: I will be the same now, more or less for ever. Most people I meet say, 'I wouldn't call you eccentric *now* . . . well, hardly'; so I know that I have moved towards the world and the world has moved towards me. We've met, at last, in a compromising position. At one time this was not so. In my Edwardian youth and Georgian middle-age the world (I mean Britain) stayed exactly where it was, aggressively conformist and conservative; I stayed exactly where I was, a blithe spirit revelling in androgynous anarchy, and there was a battle.

When I was young – before I realized that if I have any talent at all it is not for doing but for being – I dwelt in the shadows of opprobrium. I was so disfigured by the characteristics of a certain kind of homosexual person that, when I grew up, I realized that I could not ignore my predicament. I was from birth an object of mild ridicule because of my movements, especially the perpetual flutter of my hands, and my voice – which as recently as 1982 was described by a *kind* critic from *The Village Voice* (reviewing my non-performance in an off-Broadway production of Eric Bentley's *Lord Alfred's Lover*) as that of a 'nasal Mr Magoo'. I was extremely plain as a child, physically very weak, timid, dreamy, sickly, the youngest – a[1] the things for which one will never be praised.

To make matters worse, my deformative years occurred at a time when individuality was not prized and thus everything one did was criticized if it was unlike the behaviour of other people. Sometimes, with my parents, this criticism was rooted in a genuine anxiety over my future. They would think: well, he's never going to get a job wearing a pink shirt, we must explain this to him. (Then when I went on wearing a pink shirt a family row would break out.) None of this was wilful perversity on my part. Even if I had adopted the British uniform of masculinity – stoic face, stiff upper lip, obsequiously drab clothes with the fear of God tailored into them – I would have been no better equipped to deal with the world. There was never any hope that I could 'pass' as a real person. As with the character Alban, in the film *La Cage aux Folles*, disguises of normality only made me look unconvincing.

Rather than suffer the humiliation of being unmasked as a homosexual and the subject of vicious gossip; rather than be accused of creating a false impression of normality, it seemed to me preferable to be clearly identifiable as someone stranded between the sexes; an obvious *pansy*. This gave people sufficient warning and time to make up their minds as to what to do: call the police, lock up the kids, scream with laughter or duck. Possibly even to become sociable. I became not merely a self-confessed homosexual but a self-evident one. I put my case not only before the people who knew me but also before strangers. I became my own cause célèbre.

As I wrote once, in *The Naked Civil Servant*:

As soon as I put my uniform on, the rest of my life solidified around me like a plaster cast. From that moment on, my friends were anyone who could put up with the disgrace; my occupation, any job from which I was not given the sack; my playground, any café or restaurant from which I was not barred or any street from which the police did not move me on.... These crippling disadvantages gave my life an interest it would otherwise never have had. To survive at all was an adventure: to reach old age was a miracle. In one respect it was a blessing. In an expanding universe, time is on the side of the outcast. Those who once inhabited the suburbs of human contempt find that without changing their address they eventually live in the metropolis. In my case this took a very long time.

Fifty years ago, when many more people than today believed that effeminacy was synonymous with homosexuality, I mistakenly presumed that I represented homosexuality by being effeminate. Now I know that I represented nothing grander than my puny self. In recent years, as I have made many more friends among heterosexuals and been subject to attacks by gay people, this awareness – that I am first and last an individual, not a spokesman for any group – has been made all the more clear to me.

Outsiders have difficulty expressing their identities while

giving as little offence as possible. I tried personally to explain to the world that I could not help myself – that I was the victim of forces beyond my control. I certainly didn't arrive at my benighted position in life by staying awake at nights casting about for deliberate ways to annoy my parents and shock the neighbours. The difference in public attitudes towards homosexuality in the 1930s and the 1980s – I am speaking of Britain and the United States, not South Africa or Iran – is that nowadays people generally take offence only to things that are genuinely offensive – such as terrorists. In earlier times people took offence to just about *everything* that fell outside their narrow and rigid tolerances. Today most people seem to realize that 'who sleeps with whom' is just about the least of society's problems.

I have always needed the world, though at one time I was prepared to do without it. This is a well-known posture for young people: you scorn the world before it has a chance to scorn you. My entire manner was so grotesquely grand that I should think it was annoying in itself. If someone had said, 'If you go on like this you'll never have any friends,' I would have replied, haughtily and breathlessly, 'I don't care; if they don't like me as I am they can do without me.' But it isn't true. As I have remarked on many occasions: people are my only pastime. I practise no hermetic art or self-centred occupation. I am someone who *needs* some way of making my peace with the world more than others. I don't think, well, I'll just go home and build a galleon inside a bottle (*that'll* consume several anti-social years) or 'interface' with my home computer.

Exhibitionism is a drug and I was hooked on it. I needed a daily 'fix' of public consternation. I had this notion that as homosexuality was then regarded as something between a crippling disease and a poisonous fungus – smaller in its scope than Socialism but twice as deadly, especially to small children – it was my 'calling' to go about and demonstrate how *nice* a homosexual could be: kind, considerate, patient, understanding and courteous to a degree unseen in most countries outside the Orient. In short: my first impulse as a hot-blooded youth was to rebel – and, lo, I became a peacock without a cause. Eventually I realized that if I didn't want to alienate everyone by becoming more rude and shrill about my sins with every passing year (with the cause of inversion being to me what the PLO is to Vanessa Redgrave), I would have to develop a post-rebel phase to win friends and influence pulpits. It was then that I formulated Crisp's First Law: *If you feel that you cannot comply with the morality of the world you must do everything else you can to be agreeable.*

If you want to know a number of people on terms which are at least an armed truce, you have to find some way of conducting your life so that people do not attack you. If you do not want the praise, the assistance or acceptance of the world, then of course you can behave appallingly all the time and your separation from society will be mutually welcomed. People will say, 'Oh, I can't put up with him, he behaves so badly,' and you're saying, 'I don't intend to behave well, I don't need other people.' It's only when you realize that you *do* need the world – and, like me, you're on the outside looking in – that you think there *must* be some way in without abandoning your 'self'. This is what manners are: a way of getting what you want without appearing to be an absolute swine – or at least a way of getting *something* of what you want without giving total offence to other people.

When the very centre of your being – in my case, my ambiguous gender – becomes a subject of scorn, there isn't much choice about how to respond to the world: either you say, 'I'm awfully sorry, I see how wrong it is, I will not be homosexual from now onward,' or else you have to say, 'I cannot be otherwise, this is the way I am, if you can't bear it then we must never meet again.' Eventually I reasoned that even if my appearance was startling to people, everything else about me must run the other way – to minimize my breach of manners. But *this* much of my life at least must be lived on my own terms. If you are a drunkard you have to be very, very nice to people so that they are willing to see you even though they know that by the end of the evening you'll be on the floor. You've got to make yourself likeable enough to join the world in spite of your vice. Thus my interest in manners was born.

Many people, when they are young, behave badly in the

eyes of their elders but they are really only being thoughtless. I was guilty of that all the time, I was so full of hysterical energy that I was always interrupting people. I didn't actually think, Oh, what rubbish they're talking, I'm sure they'd rather listen to me; I just couldn't help myself. Now I've learned not to do this because I am totally calm and can adapt myself to any social situation much more easily. I'm not bursting to make jokes which could give offence. It's very difficult for young people not to show off – although I have known a few whose pulse was so slow that they had a reputation for being well behaved. If I am qualified to speak of manners it is because I am now an old man, the turmoil inside me has subsided and I can consider other people's feelings with equanimity.

Less than half of the remedy for bad manners consists of learning ritual. The major part consists of bringing one's self to a state of calm, whereby one needs less and isn't snatching at things or so anxious to get somewhere that one pushes other people out of the way. I feigned calm long before I actually felt it; in time the feigning of calm produced calm and calm encouraged the development of the ability to consider other people's point of view. *The Naked Civil Servant* describes the rude but necessary actions of a raw youth who felt compelled to fling down a gauntlet in the face of the world and challenge society to a duel. This book describes what I have learned since – the more important lesson of how to get along with the world and avoid dichotomies where there need be none.

Dressing as I did did not make me 'happy' necessarily, but it unified me – and that is what we must all do with our lives. There are always penalties up to any age for presenting the world with a highly individualized image, but if it is the genuine you and not some affectation (a distinction which, I realize, may take years to sort out) then you must be what you are, honestly and bravely, with all the taste and intelligence you can muster. Life will be more difficult if you try to fulfil yourself, but avoiding this difficulty renders life meaningless. To arrive at the end of your life thinking, I never did anything I *really* wanted to do ... must be one of the most profound miseries the human soul is capable of feeling – and one for which there is no last-minute cure or consolation. I have been permitted to live so long that my life has become rewarding – but that is not the reason why I made my earlier decisions, suffering low wages (I never earned more than £12 a week during my so called 'prime years') and chronic poverty, for I had no way of knowing that instead of retirement and senescence upon reaching sixty I would have a personal renaissance. In New York, where I have lived now for nearly four years, I am invited several times every week to luncheons, dinners and other social engagements with people far more famous and powerful, wealthy and wise. I have no idea what they see in me – but I am grateful for their affection and hospitality. My life has become an MGM musical full of singing, dancing and love.

If an unregenerate degenerate such as myself can reach the highest echelons of American society through the art of manners alone – and there is *nothing* else in my favour – then perhaps my observations on how to get the most out of every social transaction, for all concerned, will be instructive. If there is hope for *me* then surely there is hope for everyone.

2

Manners From Heaven

'Life begins within a family. Manners are taught and character is molded within the family structure. This is how a child learns how to cope with life. Without this knowledge, discipline, and support, the child does not grow easily into a social human being.

'Therefore, when two people marry, start a family, and reach toward their individual goals in life, they carry an enormous responsibility toward their joint creation of offspring brought into the world. It is obvious and visible to everyone that well-mannered parents raise well-mannered children. These are the people, too, who are successful in their careers and in their social lives. People with good manners care about others. They are happy people.'

Amy Vanderbilt's Everyday Etiquette revised by Letitia Baldrige*

'Charity begins at home,' Sir Thomas Browne once said, forging a cliché in the smithy of his soul. While there may be homes where charity occasionally puts in an appearance, for most of us home is the last place we would expect to find this shy woodland sprite of a virtue. We learn many things from our parents, as Hamlet can attest: abuse, deceit, vulgarity, condescension, hypocrisy, corruption, invasions of privacy, authoritarianism – and murderous rages. We do not learn 'good behaviour' in our homes except by hearsay. Living en famille provides the strongest motives for rudeness combined with the maximum opportunity for displaying it.

Embarrassment is at its most acute when it involves what an insurance broker would call 'third party risk'. Between any two people an overture can be made, a plot hatched or an insult delivered by one party and the second can reply by acquiescence or by disengaging himself without feeling or imparting a deep sense of shame. If, however, a third person is present, someone nearly always deems it necessary to explain, or, at least, excuse what has been said or done. That's the

* Doubleday, 1978.

trouble with life at home: there are too many witnesses and all of them have life-long memories.

When a movie is described as being 'family entertainment' it usually means that it depicts events and expresses sentiments that will cause no embarrassment to some members of a family if witnessed in the presence of others – providing that all members abide by a non-aggression pact in which each keeps his critical intelligence sheathed. The word 'family' as used in this phrase describes a dream unit presided over by a daughter's idea of a father, kept spick and span by a son's idea of a mother and romped in (innocently) by a parent's idea of children. It is all like a fairy tale by the brothers Grimm – but the truth is grimmer: If Mr Vincent Price were to be co-starred with Miss Bette Davis in a story by Mr Edgar Allan Poe directed by Mr Roger Corman, it could not fully express the pent-up violence and depravity of a single day in the life of the average family.

Mrs Amy Vanderbilt, an American and therefore an *optimistic* arbiter of manners, states that well-behaved parents automatically have well-behaved progeny. It could be that Mrs Vanderbilt was reading too much Mr Browne – and thinking too charitably of home. In fact, the opposite is more often true. It is in early adolescence, precisely at the age when a teen creature has begun dimly to recognize the existence of good manners, that he most dislikes his parents. He starts to react against them with the full force of his primitive nature. The only power that can control him is stark terror, but fathers with nice manners are unwilling to act forcefully. Nay, from a lifetime of feigned neutrality they have lost the knack of throwing their young across the room. This misguided lenience encourages further rebellion, and soon the parent (if a modern American) is paying $75 an hour to a psychoanalytic babysitter to 'get to the root of the problem'.

The generation now in its late – and seemingly perpetual – adolescence shocks the modern world by its nihilistic crudity. These young people were born in the sixties: they are the weed people whose parents were the older members of the flower people. Sweetness and light lead inevitably to darkness and death. If, on the other hand, its parents are tyrannical, a child tends, in self-defence, to retreat into a world of at least apparent acquiescence. In earlier times there was an alternative. The boys at least could 'run away to sea'. The sea, however, can no longer be trusted. As we know from reading the works of various Scottish poets, the sea was for ever hurt and angry, but nevertheless it represented a sort of black hole into which our more courageous misfits could disappear. Now it has been dredged by Interpol. A youngster has hardly set foot upon some foreign strand before the police seize him and return him to his parents. The authorities have not yet realized that the one place to which those who have run away from home must on no account be returned is their point of departure.

The primary impoliteness of many parents is their failure to conceal the fact that to them their children are not individuals; they are simply their ambassadors to the world. As soon as a son hears his mother begin a sentence with the words, 'I never thought that any child of mine ...' he knows that she is not for a moment interested in his happiness; she is only concerned with how he represents her to the neighbours. He is not being brought up; he is being published by the directors of a household of which he is, however reluctantly, a product. His wishes can never be the point of an argument – though at home there will be little else but discord.

Can any rules be constructed that will act as a breakwater to this tide of bitterness? Parents must learn to treat their children as equals in all matters that do not concern worldly wisdom. Sometimes even *that* can be explained. A schoolgirl committed a minor crime which some busybody brought to the notice of the headmistress. The child's mother was summoned to the school and the situation explained to her. The parent expressed herself in agreement with the proposed punishment. Later, at home, the daughter protested; she had assumed that her mother would be on her side. 'While you attend that school, I shall always appear to be in agreement with your teachers because I pay no fees for your education.' Thus the child was not given an unbelievable po-faced lecture about morality but a glimpse of the world that she would soon enter as it really is. In that moment she was treated by her mother as an equal – although a nuisance.

As a child I had great difficulty trying to work out what *natural* behaviour was in any aspect of human life. How could I explain to my parents that I was an extraterrestrial destined to take his manners from heaven? My father disliked me and I returned the compliment, my mother was a failed Lady Bracknell. My father died when I was twenty-two, my mother never understood my activities as a model or a freelance commercial artist and until she died (when I was fifty-six) she would say, 'Are you still out of work?'

In my early years of acute embarrassment (otherwise known as 'childhood'), I didn't *know* that I was a resident alien: that adjustment to society was maladjustment for *me*. Alternately I confirmed and denied what was set forth, alternately I protested and acquiesced: this is what happens to most young people – one day they decide to brazen out their individuality, the next they decide that the price is too great and they try to conform. It may take years for someone to realize that they are miscast for the roles they are offered in the Broadway drama of Life, and that they would be better off declining a part in an overrated mediocrity. There are great roles off-Broadway.

Doubtless this realization comes earlier to some people than to others. In my case, it wasn't until I was nearly thirty that I brought to an end the anguish of failing to conform, of not measuring up to other people's expectations. The biggest single obstacle I faced was that I was genuinely and absolutely unable to understand other people's feelings and point of view even when it was forcibly expressed, and as a result I couldn't make the correct gestures towards them. I can remember during the war being totally unable to understand why people would walk around Chelsea going to bomb sites and watching them being dismantled in search of bodies. I remember one woman saying to me, when I'd joined a huddle of observers for a moment, 'For heaven's sake, don't look as if you're enjoying yourself.' And I said, 'All right,' and put on a grave appearance, like hers, as if contemplating mortality from a poetical point of view (as opposed to the commercial view of an undertaker). Yet inwardly I was flummoxed as to why anyone should go to a bomb site and reverentially stare at people searching for dead bodies in a great hole in the ground. *Apparently* it was natural for this woman (and many others) to go there, although she couldn't let it appear that she was morbidly excited.

Throughout my life I've never been able to understand other people's reactions to *anything*, which makes it harder for me to do and say the 'natural' thing. Now, if told of somebody's death, I will say, 'How terrible . . .' and look at the floor for an appropriate interval, but I don't really feel it is terrible because in my view death is the *least* awful thing that can happen to someone. A great many human sentiments strike me as the bad habits of a conditioned psyche rather than what a person truly feels or thinks. I don't empathize with others' concern with 'world issues' or 'moral problems'. I have never voted: all political parties are the same once they take office, and I don't see the point of voting for redundancy. I've lived under Conservative governments and Labour governments in England for nearly seventy years without altering my way of living in the least. Ideally the purpose of government is to create a walled garden in which anarchy can flourish. *Wise* governments have frayed edges; as if to say: these are the rules but they're probably not absolute. Unwise governments (run by parties that take themselves too seriously) tend to say: these are the rules, fixed for ever, and we'll enforce them with all our might. Something is bound to go wrong. Human nature invalidates every form of government – and the form that it invalidates the fastest is totalitarianism. Had there been a Surrealist Party I might have voted for that. I certainly felt that my life in England fulfilled the basic definition of surrealism: the absurd juxtaposition of two objects not normally found together.

Once, when I was in a railway carriage stuffed with teachers, on my way to the Maidstone School of Art where I was employed as a model, someone asked for my opinion about modern art. It was at a time in my life when I still rashly spoke my mind. I said I'd never understood art of any kind, and I meant it. Whereupon one of the masters said, 'That's no answer, because you have made of yourself a work of art – maybe a bad work of art – but all the same, you are a conscious creation and have thought about not only your appearance but also your entire way of life, your mode of speaking, your gestures, the way you live. You've done all this exactly like someone standing in front of a canvas, saying, "The pink is too bright, I'll tone it down a little." You have rearranged yourself until you are the best you can do with the poor materials available.' (He didn't actually say *that* but that's what he meant.) It was then that I realized that I had indeed become my own creation – not merely noticed by others but recognized for what I was. I was suffused with a feeling of relief – as if at last I had crossed a bridge from muddled youth to self-confident maturity.

People tend to be born with everything in turmoil inside them and they have to keep pushing it around to get to a point where they are comfortable; once they succeed in that and overcome a kind of 'moral indigestion' they begin to feel calmer and are able to address the world with less anxiety and greater patience. Anything that assists one in arriving at a calm state in life – yoga, exercise, meditation by the sea and, above all else, having a room of one's own, a place where no one intrudes – will probably have a beneficial effect on one's manners. I think that one does want less as the years go by, but even if this were not so one takes a longer view of the world and one's relation to it. There isn't this desperate need to have something or prove something *now*. Instead you think: well, I'll think about it and if tomorrow I still feel as strongly as this I will set about dealing with the situation. Once you realize that some of your reactions are immediate and temporary (and not worth making a fuss about), you have already won half the battle. This process might be termed 'temperamental exercises': you begin to temper your judgements and judge your tempers for your own sake as well as for others'.

Once you have decided who you are, even for the time being, and sorted out your real needs from your apparent, immediate ones, you can then present to the world this considered image in a considered manner. The more sure you are of yourself, of your image, of how you see yourself, of what the overall message of your existence is, the more calm your way of expressing yourself becomes. When you are a child, or are childish, you tend to live in a fragmented but all-consuming dream of yourself so that your mercurial joys, griefs and worries are something you can't help imposing upon others. There are insensitive people who stand beside you at a bus stop and within two minutes they're saying, 'I'll never get there, these buses never come, I've been late for an appointment twice this week.' Such people *can't* think: this person beside me is probably just as anxious as I am, the bus is just as late for him, I shouldn't impose my problems. It isn't that those people have a message, or anything else, to give you: they are so full of themselves that other people barely exist. Children and animals behave in much the same way, exploding with useless energy: dogs rush into a room and jump all over you, they don't know *how* to think: they don't want to be covered in dog hair, I should creep in and lie quietly in a corner. Children burst into a room where their mother is playing bridge and demand attention to some tale that no one wants to hear – least of all at that moment. Low forms of life and the immature live in a constant state of self-centred turmoil.

Gradually, for those who aspire to learn the tao of manners, the time comes when you settle what your limits are: you begin to look inward – *and* outward. You may think, as I did: well, it's all a mess inside but it's the best I can do and I won't go on about it any more. With that settled you begin to look outward, and when someone arrives and says, 'I've broken my wrist,' you *don't* reply, 'Oh, I can imagine it's terrible, I remember a time when I broke my *entire* arm, and I was in a cast ...' You're able to say, simply, 'Is there anything I can do?'

At some point in my early thirties I began to take a conscious interest in my behaviour and to study that of others with a keen but detached interest. As I knew more and more people and began to live the 'café life', I would spend time most days with strangers, and if not strangers, with the merest of acquaintances; that's when your manners count for most because *that's* all they see, they can't really form a view of your character. You are simply somebody whom they would or would not like to have sit with them. I remember a certain Mrs McAllister saying, 'You're crazy about your entrance aren't you?' And I said, 'What do you mean?' knowing quite well what she meant and secretly pleased that she had noticed. I had only to arrive and people would be saying, 'Come and sit with us.' I used to have my soup at one table, my entrée at another, my coffee at a third – because I can never have too many people. That's when you cultivate a certain public image in a small way: you want to seem interesting to look at, to phrase things interestingly and amusingly, and above all else, to seem to be concerned with other people.

I made a deliberate decision about this.

Learning about people is rather like reading a book; you have to try to remember what you read last week. Nothing is more effective than to be able to sit down at someone's table and say, 'How's your broken heart?' Or, 'How's your rheumatism?' This wins over people like nothing else, although it is only a feat of memory.

I have remained all my life a resident alien in the heart of the world (immune to most human problems – but subject to a few special difficulties). I have thus learned to be an agreeable companion to many different people of all ages and stages in life, genuinely interested in almost everybody as long as they don't repeat themselves. There is an important distinction to be made between taking an interest in people and in becoming emotionally involved. I adore the former and avoid the latter. I am genuinely able to take an interest in subjects that have no pertinence to my life. Let's say, your cat becomes ill; now *I* would simply put it in a basket, take it to a vet and say get rid of the damn thing. But I will take an interest in why on earth *you* care so deeply about your cat. It's interesting even though I have no feelings about the creature. I don't sympathize in the true sense of the word, I do not lay my feelings alongside yours in maudlin rapport, but I take an interest in things that are important to others as a further revelation of human nature.

I may think: how extraordinary for a grown-up to be going through this crisis over a cat. Has this person nothing else in his life but his cat? Or is it that his cat's ailment is the only thing he feels free to share with me? And so on. As a well-mannered listener to your dogmas and catastrophes, I bring an engagement and a detachment at the same time. My interest is real (if somewhat ironic), but I won't burst into tears if your furry loved one dies. In my youth my 'lack of feelings' and 'uncertainties of how to react' to people were one of my torments, but once I stopped measuring myself by other people and abstract standards, I found that these aspects of my personality were useful in producing placidity.

If I had to give one explanation for other people's problems it would be: 'I-love-you-more-than-you-love-me.' I have not felt this in the last fifty years. If I love you, I love you and I am concerned to find ways of expressing this that will not be a burden to you. I was horrified one night at the Players Theater on MacDougal Street in Greenwich Village, New York. While performing in the show, *An Evening With Quentin Crisp*, the subject of love came up and a woman said, 'One loves surely in the hope of being loved in return?' I couldn't help answering, though it was bad manners to do so, 'That is a terrible thing to say.' This is the heart of any number of people's problems: they want their love to be requited – which seems to me to be completely beside the point. Love doesn't have to be requited to be called love. This key problem which disfigures many lives happily does not affect me in the least. Lonely people are empty people. It is an evasion of responsibility to one's self to hope that someone else will come along and fill the black holes of your soul.

Manners are love in a cool climate. If I had one message to beam to the human race it would be: Cool it – and start treating one another better than you do in heat.

3

Mortal Coils

'Perhaps nothing is so depressing an index of the inhumanity of the male supremacist mentality as the fact that the more genial human traits are assigned to the female underclass: affection, response to sympathy, kindness, cheerfulness and politeness.'

Kate Millett, *Sexual Politics*

The 1980s are great years for individuality but a disaster for manners. The fact that society attaches less importance to conformity now than in earlier decades is due mainly to the battering ram of youthful iconoclasm which has been banging away for twenty-five years at the doors of law, morality and culture. Ever since the postwar baby boom entered puberty en masse, the young have not been so much an intellectual influence upon Western culture as a brute statistical force. Adolescence is not renowned for its subtlety or social grace, and this libidinous explosion upon Western society had the effect of raising the sexual temperature of popular culture and lowering the tone of daily life.

Who should know better than I, a beneficiary of this erosion of standards? As I saunter through the streets of New York's Lower East Side keeping alive the low-rent literary traditions of the Beat Generation, the fact that people come up to me and ask for my autograph instead of throwing stones as they did in England is a sure sign of social decay. It is much less of a conflict to be an individual now, but that is because standards of all kinds – moral, aesthetic, intellectual – have been suspended. The death and disappearance of You-Know-Who was a great blow to mankind's mental security, though that security rested upon a naïve cosmology as fragile as a dandelion clock. Religious doubts and moral turmoil have been compounded in recent decades by the militant rise of all sorts of minorities demanding their 'rights'. The revolt of the young against all forms of authority, the emergence of feminism as a potent political philosophy and the accelerated rate of change in all phases of human life has militated towards such a social maelstrom that it's a wonder we get so much as a polite nod at the bus queue.

This freedom is a mixed blessing. It's easier for the likes of me to go about unmolested, but it's harder to get attentive service in department stores, or to be given a seat with generous gallantry on the tube or bus. The same wave of indifference that washed me in washed a lot of good things out.

This venture I have undertaken – of defining decorum in the post-Freudian age and suggesting preferable ways of behaving in all sorts of perilous situations – is prompted by a concern that there is no truly sophisticated guide to modern manners in existence and, what is worse, there is widespread scepticism towards whether manners matter any more. A woman I met recently in New York typifies this viewpoint: she is a well-to-do, Jewish divorcee with three daughters all in both their early twenties and analysis. The mother has aspirations towards genteelism (in the arts if not everyday life), but the result is rather like a fishwife putting on airs. Her daughters are *laissez-faire* wildflowers undirected by any master gardener. All three have live-in boyfriends (sad characters even more slovenly than the young women), two of the girls have had abortions, and one has a serious drug problem. None of these matters are exactly a violation of manners but the fact that they are openly talked about to the acute embarrassment of anyone who would rather not know is. Foul language is permitted but not condoned. Mother will say, 'I wish you wouldn't speak like that at the dinner table,' and her youngest daughter will retort, 'That's too f**king bad!' Family gatherings such as Thanksgiving or Passover usually begin on a lofty note, with fresh-cut flowers, the best china, and two days' of artful cooking on display – but somewhere between the first and last courses, bits and pieces of dirty laundry are dragged out, no matter who else is present, and soon the air becomes a Pinteresque mixture of

L'air du Temps and recrimination (to say nothing of the whiffs of Tigerbalm, a most aggressive fragrance, which the youngest daughter is addicted to, and which overwhelms every other scent within a ten-foot radius). It was the mother of this horror-movie brood who said to me after a brawling family reunion, 'I'm afraid I don't see the point to a book on manners. I don't think anyone has a formula to cover all situations.' (Her mocking smile said, 'Least of all – you.') 'We just have to improvise as best we can.' A minute later she was back in the fray, improvising at the top of her voice. Then she ran to her bedroom and burst into tears. It may seem simplistic to suggest that this family's persistent problems in understanding and communication could be alleviated by good manners, but a family in which no one is willing to assume the responsibility of clarifying what good behaviour is, is one in which no one will recognize good behaviour when it occurs, no one aims at it, so no one feels any dismay about failing to achieve it. The reasons for this particular family's problems may be complex, but the basic failure is a common one in America in that it is run by its younger members with no leadership (only sympathy alternating with exasperation) from its single parent and sole authority.

If we are foolish enough to regard the young as our mentors in anything (except, perhaps, for their pioneering research in chemical derangement – frequently and paradoxically coupled with a zealous interest in 'health foods'), the last thing we can consult them on is good behaviour, a phrase which, for most of them, has no meaning outside of reformatories (one gets 'time off' for 'good behaviour'). Caught up as they are in the mortal coils of youth, they are not only likely to be inconsiderate about most things but to rationalize their rudenesses as revolutionary. This problem can be alleviated considerably by the way that older people conduct themselves in dealing with the young.

For example: 'It's been lovely having you over for a drink, but I'm afraid we're going to settle down now for our evening meal.' Such a pointed remark (practically an arrow at the door) may offend a young guest or embarrass him, but at least they have not placed him in a position where he can do the wrong thing and overstay his welcome. There is something askew, and certainly inefficient, in letting people stay until four in the morning and then saying: 'I thought they would never go!' It's up to you to get rid of them at an hour you won't resent and thus end up speaking badly of them.

Never say to anyone who is less than twenty-five, 'Drop in any time, because that person may be back *tomorrow*, reading more hospitality into your words than you meant. They may have been brought up in such a way that they don't recognize that most conversations are a series of formalities. I'm sure I've been guilty of unexpectedly visiting people who'd said, 'Drop in any time,' without realizing that that was English for 'Goodbye'. Or that I've stayed hours too long, or held forth on a subject that other people only wanted to touch upon, or flatly contradicted people (because as a young man I used to take up half-baked ideas with an irrepressible passion). Older people should at all times, when dealing with those who are younger, set clear guidelines and limits: you might be resented but that is preferable to being abused. Most young people have little sense of what constitutes 'appropriate' behaviour, and any decision affecting the interests of someone who is older (and marginally wiser) should not be left to the indiscretion of the indiscriminate.

It isn't just the parents trying to be 'buddies' with their children who bestow upon the young inordinate power. A large number of middle-aged adults have come to feel that their lives – which revolve around work and the earning of money – are hollow and meaningless, whereas young masters of hedonism and mistresses of play are regarded as being full of wholesome vitality, to be envied and, worse, emulated.

Whenever one meets a middle-aged man with his shirt unbuttoned to his navel, sporting a three-ring circus of ostentatious jewellery around his neck and wearing trousers so tight that his religion is revealed, one may be sure that he has imbibed too often at the fountain of youth. Even worse than this sartorial attempt to be 'with it' is the profoundly pathetic attempt by an older person to adopt the vocabulary, habits and tastes of the young.

I recently met one of these unfelicitous hybrids – a cross between an old goat and a pseudo-teen – whose life story would have to be called the 'Tragedy of a Ridiculous Man'.

This Canadian gentleman rang me up as so many other people do (I feel I owe it to the world to live with a listed telephone number) and introduced himself with a beguilingly cosmopolitan air. He asked me to attend his fifty-first birthday party, deep in the verdant countryside of western Ontario. He offered to pay my expenses in exchange for my presence. I said, 'I want what you want' – a phrase which I have used throughout my adult life after discovering my true nothingness. It causes my agent to shudder as it leads to all sorts of strange assignations.

At the metaphorical border of Customs and Immigration at Toronto International Airport I was startled to hear an immigration official say, upon checking my passport, 'Vindicated at last, eh?' (The upturned 'eh' is a species of linguistic dim-witticism to which Canadians are addicted.) I muttered, 'You're too kind,' and moved on. There were so many people lined up to get through the gates of Toronto one would think that the city fathers were offering free citizenship to the first 500 refugees who could answer a skill-testing question.

There was nothing in the appearance or manner of my host to prompt apprehensiveness, but I have learned through a long lifetime of variegated experiences to regard blandness as the most suspect front of all. Most people are fakes: they're like plastic tables covered in rosewood veneer; it doesn't take much to make them peel and crack and reveal the inferior substance at their core. It was not a surprise, therefore, when my host began a voluble conversation, as we drove to his pastoral hideaway 100 miles away, by appraising the relative merits of various recordings of *The Mikado* only to end up relating extremely tasteless anecdotes from his personal life. While my responses became fastidiously briefer and then fatuously noncommittal, his vocabulary and range of interests steadily declined until finally his conversation came to resemble an elevator plunging straight to hell – whizzing past the levels of 'Rabelaisian', 'Petronian', 'Millerian' (Henry), 'contemporary low comic', and 'moronically vulgar', down into the bottomless pits of scatology.

By the time he confessed to having a criminal record – first for a conviction in a marijuana 'bust' in the early 1970s, and secondly, for an act of 'gross indecency' with an under-age

male student at the college where he once taught – I realized
that I was in the presence of a man of pitifully poor
judgement. He railed against 'the establishment' like a
disgruntled teenager; having been raised in a stuffy family in
England he had found the 'permissiveness' of North America
greatly to his liking. He regarded himself as a liberated free
spirit who was demonstrating to society that homosexuality
was not a curse, yet he had contrived to live his life in such a
way that homosexuality was clearly a tragic flaw. He described being beaten up on several occasions by 'fag-bashers'
he had ill-advisedly propositioned in a rural redneck pub; he
described how he once picked up two teenaged hitch-hikers
and how one of them robbed him while he was dallying with
the other and he had frequently been saddled with near-
moronic houseguests – waifs and layabouts who moved in
after he had 'tricked' with them. It was clear, even without
the corroborating evidence that followed, that here was
another victim of the sexual revolution – a *sexaholic*: a man
whose attachment to sex is as compulsive and mechanical as
an alcoholic's addiction to booze.

The problem I faced was how to endure a weekend without
giving offence to a man whom I could not respect. His house,
it turned out, was a seventy-year-old church. Where once
there had been a picture of the Madonna and child over the
altar there was now a graphically explicit oil painting of five
men having an orgy. It was a first painting by a young artist,
my host explained to me while I stared ahead but inwardly
averted my gaze, a depiction of events that supposedly
happened frequently in a 'cruising' park on Mount Royal in
Montreal. 'The cops will crack down on it some day and spoil
all our fun,' he said, sounding like a naughty boy who *wants*
to be caught. Outside the church, where there had once been
a cross over the front door, there was now a string of pink
lights arranged into a triangle. A pink triangle, he informed
me, was a symbol of 'homosexual oppression'. It struck me as
a symbol of bad taste. The washroom walls were covered with
lewd adolescent graffiti, baleful evidence of the influence of
the young which pervaded the place. Most of the other guests
who arrived that night were from a place called Chatham.
The music was vacuous, with a percolating synthesizer used

to plug the holes of the melodic deficiencies, it was played so loudly that its supposed artistic value was rendered beyond judgement. Once again I reflected that quite possibly the worst part of being gay in the twentieth century is all the damn disco music to which one has to listen. At one point my host shrugged apologetically in my direction, as if to say, 'What can I do: *They* love it.' Sophistication was now in full retreat and adulthood was waving a white flag. His thralldom with youth had turned his home into a living version of the film *Animal House* where good taste had been banished in the name of liberating the senses from pious restraints, and where perpetually immature people thought that breaking wind was as funny as a line by Noel Coward.

On the pretext that I was old and tired I managed to excuse myself from the festivities just as my host was about to show porn-movies to the crowd. In fairness to anyone who objects to my view that the influence of the young is deleterious in most areas of social behaviour, I should say that one young man came up to me and said, 'The only reason I came here tonight was to meet you, Mr Crisp. I'm sorry that you made a trip from New York only to be exposed to all this grossness.' Here and there among the young, one finds the nascent mutation of good manners, the dawn of consciousness but, generally, because adolescence is full of weird and unwelcome bodily changes, young people are obsessed with physical details. Instead of the suppression of the physical self, something which good manners require, the young never miss an opportunity to refer to 'barfing', 'farting', 'oozing' and 'burping' and all the other ways that the human body can be offensive.

In the morning, applying a second coat of whitewash to my manners, I explained to my host that I was feeling mildly ill and ought to return home to New York where I could rest properly. I was effusive in my thanks for his hospitality, and prostrate with regret that my stay could not be longer (my bags were already packed). At the airport he bid adieu by saying, 'Well, it's been a slice, eh? I hope you'll come back real soon and if ever I'm in New York . . .' 'There are plenty of places there to interest a man of your taste,' I replied. I mustered my remaining strength to offer a smile of utter fatuity, then hightailed it back to my New York room where I had a good cry and then did four crossword puzzles in a row to restore some sense of civilization.

This man's example, while extreme, is not irrelevant. In some degree a great many people have responded in a similar fashion to the influence of the young (beginning in the 1960s) and loosened their stays, unbuttoned their libidos, unzipped their psyches, and little by little, more and more, let informality reign in all areas of life. They stopped asking, 'Do you mind if I smoke?' and began taking it for granted that no one would mind because in the world of the young nobody minds anything if it can be rationalized as being pleasurable. Cigarette smoking gave way to casual pot smoking. Increasing informality among men and women lead to couples fondling and caressing each other in public – not because they were oblivious to those around them but, even more inconsiderately, because they *wanted* to have an audience to see that they were – for an hour, a week, or a year – 'lovers'. With some people it became mandatory to advertise every detail of their sexual behaviour constantly. To the young, forcing others to watch or listen – be they friends, family members or complete strangers – is the next best thing to being on television. In recent years this trend towards dispensing with formalities has become stronger and is today the main threat to our achieving a more polite society in the future. What is at stake here is not mere decorum but efficiency in a wide range of social relations. A society in which 'anything goes' is one in which nothing goes well.

In addition to the scepticism and rebellion of the young where 'rules and regulations' are concerned, a second force – the rise of feminism – has now dovetailed with the first, causing manners to deteriorate even faster and more completely. I do not mean to suggest that feminists are in error (though in my view a sex that wants 'equality' with men can only be levelling downward) or that their goals are on a par with the shortsighted whims of youth, but rather that the ironic side effect of women having abandoned their privileged status as 'ladies' is that they are now in danger of being as revolting as men, and accordingly treated, by men, as nothing special.

The manners of modern man have fallen in a post-feminist slump; the relationship between men and women has become a kind of mutual rape. Men have not rid themselves of the Victorian notion that courtesy was a way of treating ladies – and ladies are on the way out. There is an unalterable law that if one group envies another it will, given half a chance, imitate the *worst* characteristics of the admired species. Now one finds certain women smoking in the streets, swearing at the police and competing with men in every phase of life with all the social graces of a Medusa; it is not because they have found the true, unfettered nature of woman but because they have adopted such appalling role-models.

For those who were born yesterday, or simply act that way from watching too much television, with no experience or knowledge of the past, a mini-history of the relations between the sexes may be useful here. Those whose memories go back to the Middle Ages may skip this section.

In medieval times a knight worshipped his lady from afar. (It *is* the easiest way.) Sometimes he never even spoke to her in his entire life. Nevertheless, she remained the sole inspiration for his bravery and for her sake he fought until he died, frequently travelling to foreign lands and engaging in battles to the outcome of which he was generally totally indifferent. So great a degree of self-sacrifice now seems to us far-fetched – almost Polish. Since those days, the attitude of men towards women has fluctuated considerably. During the reign of Queen Elizabeth I, the lamp of chivalry burned brightly and the female sex was revered. Mr Phillip Sidney went so far as to begin one of his sonnets with the appeal, 'O world, be nobler for her sake.' In Stuart times, the image of women became tougher and it was not until a female monarch ascended the throne (in 1837) that women once again became sacred.

Victorianism has now become a term of abuse; many women nowadays feel that it was a time of bondage for their sex. If a woman suffered from fierce appetites or strong ambitions this may have been so, but it is hard to imagine a period of English history when women of the middle classes enjoyed a more privileged position. Good manners in the nineteenth century were almost entirely a question of behaving deferentially in the presence of ladies. What does it matter that men put women on pedestals for the same reason that restaurateurs put chairs on tables – to get them out of the way while making a clean sweep of things? Their susceptibilities were thought to be exquisite. When a girl (of his own class, of course) entered a room, a gentleman, if he was not to be thought an absolute cad, had to rise and find her a seat. This must never be the one on which he had been sitting for fear that it may have been warmed by his person. How delicious to be thought capable of feeling anything through all those petticoats, but, even at the time, a lady wrote to a friend, 'A woman would have to be a veritable ghost to be able to comply with present standards of decorum.'

I suppose that Victorian women resented the strictures placed upon their natures, but never again will there be a society which bestows on them, in the social and domestic senses, so large a realm of which they are the absolute monarchs. During the middle part of the last century, etiquette became as complicated as a cotillion. Visiting cards flew through the air like snowflakes on a windy winter's day. This seems to have been a world invented entirely by women and enjoyed at least by some. Men married in order to leave the management of 'the social whirl' to their wives. Most books on etiquette were written by women for women. Good manners – like other refined aspects of life, such as taking an interest in ballet or the opera – were considered to be part of a woman's contribution to civilization.

Domestic chores, cooking, blowing the noses and wiping the bottoms of children are far nastier occupations than the making of money, so it is obvious that almost from birth most women have been plunged into a more revolting side of life than men, but the notion that women are the more refined species has lingered on – and in the hearts of the most unlikely people. Marcel Proust, whose view of human nature was by no means sanguine, once said to Celeste, his last and most faithful housekeeper, 'Your father was a good man but goodness, even in the best of men, can never be what it is in a woman. There is always a layer of roughness. A man can never be goodness itself.'

For men, the way to avoid having to behave nicely all the

time was to leave the company of the opposite sex for as long as possible. This practice will one day be known as the Australian solution. Apparently it also prevailed in Cincinnati in the 1820s – where escapees from etiquette gathered to start another brash 'new world' town. During that decade, Mrs Trollope, the English authoress, paid the city a prolonged visit in order to build a vast emporium. The venture was a total failure. Illogically her anger fell not upon herself but on the entire American nation. In her book, *The Domestic Manners of Americans*, Mrs Trollope complains of almost everything, but in particular of the habits of the men. They chewed tobacco, they spat, they gambled and their language was coarse. In order to pursue these occupations freely and without shame, they chose the company of one another rather than that of their womenfolk. Mrs Trollope objected to this because she didn't like the exclusive society of women; she felt that, in America, they were 'guarded by a sevenfold shield of insignificance'.

In this century the difference between the sexes is diminishing. For this reason good manners are also vanishing. As women have become more aggressive and less refined, many men seem to have been driven to adopt still cruder tastes in order to preserve some vestige of a masculine image. The implication is that such men identify 'maleness' with 'roughness', one step away from utter beastliness. As women have been perceived as becoming more 'masculine' these beleaguered men have taken to cultivating the 'ultra-masculine' and indulging in all kinds of violent activity.

This is especially sad because it is needless. In many areas of human activity we have moved into an era when the great physical strength often associated with M. Proust's 'layer of roughness' is no longer necessary. Millions of men could now live enjoyable, productive lives and make use of all their skills without so much as getting their fingernails dirty. This advance of civilization they do not welcome; they resent it. Some have even stopped eating quiche – though apparently 'real' men will continue to consume all the separate ingredients (eggs, cheese, cream, and the like) that go into making quiches: their confused sense of manhood preserved by mere sleight-of-hand and the thinnest of illusions.

It was not always so.

Classical and even medieval works on deportment make little or no mention of the special treatment of women. There was a time when, though noblemen urinated along the corridors of Versailles, courteousness – even elaborate flourishes of behaviour – were offered for their own sake. Then it was not only the presence of a supposed 'gentle sex' that provoked good behaviour; good behaviour was also the outward sign of a civilized nature, conscious of its social obligations to all human beings. We may be glad that all that visiting card rubbish has subsided but we must remember that, just as rituals are essential to religion, so good manners are essential if we are to consider the feelings of others.

Perhaps because I have lived my life between the sexes and never developed an exaggerated mythology about either I have not felt inclined to radically alter my behaviour towards men or women simply because they behave differently from the way they once did, or their parents did. As my attitude towards women is based on the recognition that they are an *apposite* sex of fellow human beings, not an opposite sex of incomprehensible creatures, my manners have not slipped into a slough of male despond.

If you partake, consciously, of the nature of both sexes, then you may develop a romantic attitude rather than merely a sexual attitude; that is, you will treat both men and women as people rather than as things and offer to both sexes your most thoughtful and gallant behaviour. I regard women as not necessarily frailer than myself, that's hardly possible, especially at my age, but more precious and valuable. So if I were to hold my umbrella over a woman to keep her dry rather than myself it would be because she was more worth keeping dry than I am. In my romantic view, she may be a princess or the richest woman in the world but she can never be more than a lady. There is a sense in which I always try to treat women as though they had to be 'looked after', but when I am with men I have the romantic view that *they* will look after me. Indeed only a few days ago a radio interviewer said that when he had walked through the streets with me at dawn to get a taxi to go to our interview, he had felt responsible for me. I now, almost automatically, present myself to men as someone who is helpless, hopeless, and must at any moment be cosseted, protected or merely guided and advised. While my attitude towards men is different from my attitude towards women, it is equally romantic, and in both cases I fancy it has the aim and often the effect of bringing out the best in people. Even in the worst of people. The point at which I first realized how important manners can be is superbly depicted in the television play based on *The Naked Civil Servant* (starring John Hurt). There's a moment when I'm fairly badly beaten by several young men in the streets of London; I lean against a wall, covered with blood and I say, 'I seem to have offended you gentlemen in some way.' That actually stopped them. It made the whole situation so ludicrous that they laughed – genuine laughter, not merely mocking laughter. I literally saved my life with good manners.

There have been several occasions since when people have rung me up and threatened to kill me, and I have said, 'Would you like an appointment? Let me see when I can fit you in.' Thus I show that I've heard what they said and responded politely but I've also shown that I don't really believe them. Now one day I may be wrong, they may keep the appointment and they may kill me, but that would easily be worth it because, at my age, death is much less worrying than taxes. In situations such as these, where manners mask your fear or actually overcome your fear, or in less trying situations where manners are called upon to mask your fatigue with people, then I would say that they triumph: they become a uniquely civilized, non-violent tool for dealing with a wide range of intrusions. Good manners won't cure illnesses nor remedy poverty, but they are the only way of coping with most social problems and solving some of them.

Now that we have an armed vision – and will be on guard against Creeping Sloppiness (the leading philosophy of the young) and the Fall of Woman (in the eyes of man) – we can proceed to create not more 'laws' of etiquette (which are bound to become outmoded in a world of rapid change) but a flexible and adaptable method of behaving in a complex society. As someone accustomed to occupying the middle ground in all aspects of life beginning with the sexual, it seems clear that we must chart a course between the fuddy-duddy strictures of yesterday and the hapless chaos of today. Whenever you're in doubt about what to do – trust a man in the middle. You may not go far, but the consolation is that you won't go far wrong.

First I propose a crash course in Crisperanto, otherwise known as manners of speaking; learning to mislead your foes – which is practically everybody (remember, Jean-Paul Sartre once said, 'Hell is other people') – with Machiavellian aplomb. Crisperanto is the art of speaking with such guile, subtlety and duplicity that an opponent never knows what seduced him. You will need a copy of Machiavelli's *The Prince* and a good dictionary: now let us pry.

4

The Art of Crisperanto

'Considering manners even in their superficial
aspect, no one – unless he be a recluse who comes in
contact with no other human being – can fail to reap
the advantage of a proper, courteous and likeable
approach, or fail to be handicapped by an improper,
offensive and resented one.'

Emily Post, *Etiquette*

When I was a child the only time I felt united with my
brothers and my sister was when someone was present who
attracted more ridicule than I. One such victim was a little
girl with a pronounced squint. At a party we all teased her so
much that she ran and appealed to my mother with the
question, 'My eyes aren't different, are they?' My mother
replied, 'Each is beautiful in its own way.'

Tact is a major branch of manners. It depends less on a
standard of behaviour that can be learned in childhood than
upon a huge vocabulary and an ingenious mind accustomed
to dealing with the vagaries of human behaviour, from the
surly curmudgeon who broods blackly in his bile to the sunny
young lady upon whose countenance naïvety glistens like a
dewdrop.

Human nature is trickier stuff to handle than liquid
nitrogen. It sometimes appears safe and solid but is likely to
turn into a combustible gas at any moment. Learning to say
the right thing, when one's audience is so diverse, and
sometimes perverse, is an art for which there are few general
rules. One learns by climbing a social ladder where every rung
is slippery.

When I lived in England I knew a woman who would say
something like, 'Such a nice day, I think we should go out.'
And I would say, 'All right.'

'Shall we walk by the river?' she would ask. I would humbly follow, saying, 'Yes.'

'Oh – look at the swans,' she would say. I would look, and reply, 'Yes.'

Then one day in the midst of what I took to be an agreeable stroll, she turned to me and said, 'You never do *anything* with enthusiasm!' and I said, 'Uhm, no....' So I came to realize that too much calm is offputting to most people (though I like nothing better than a luxurious wallow in indifference) and that, for their sake, one should add a bit of colour to one's conversation. Now if someone were to say, 'Such a nice day, I think we should go out,' I would reply, 'I was hoping you would suggest that.' Then if she said, 'Shall we walk by the river?' I would reply, 'Oh, it's one of my favourite walks.' And when she said, 'Look at the swans,' I would reply, 'Aren't they marvellous?' This gives people the feeling they are doing things right; you are praising them in praising the world.

It was through many such experiences that 'Crisperanto' was created. Crisperanto is a manner of speaking in which a sentence gets all dressed up to create a pleasing impression. It wears a bit more eyeshadow, rouge and lipstick than is absolutely necessary (some people may even say, 'That's laying it on a bit thick') and then it saunters forth, or if it is witty it sallies, to lightly amuse a jaded world. Unlike Esperanto, which reduces several European languages to their common denominators with the aim of producing a basic vocabulary of simple words and concepts, Crisperanto is composed of a rainbow of words – from the arcane treasures of antiquity to the latest slang from video-dens of iniquity. It is speaking with a courtly flourish – artificial and insincere like all the best things in life, but charming. Its sole purpose is to mislead people into thinking that one takes an affable interest in anything they say or do – which pleases them and costs one nothing – thus keeping the social machinery oiled and working efficiently.

It is best to begin all conversations by being bland – rather than witty or what Americans call 'smart'. You start in a very general way with anyone you haven't met before, or know from experience is likely to feel at a loss socially; your words should convey that you take a mild interest in meeting them

– nothing that will startle an antelope-soul. You must never blind anyone with your cleverness or your education. To be on the safe side here you should cultivate your betters rather than your inferiors at every opportunity – that way you'll resist the temptation to score easy victories over those who are not your equals. Never start off a conversation with a girl who looks absolutely terrified with a quotation from Ovid, but if, upon further acquaintance, she turns out to be a classical scholar then of course you may quote Latin until it almost becomes a living language again. Having begun by serving the thinnest of conversational consommé, you proceed with care to add more substantial ingredients, a few spices, even a dash of sherry. If successful, you will create a savoury soup-for-two; if not, you will end up eating your words in another sense.

It is easier to be well mannered with people that one can *see*; inasmuch as one has chosen to meet them by attending a certain social gathering. In the parlance of the young, one is 'psyched-up' to the ordeal of civility. The invention of the telephone, however, enables people to barge into our homes at the most awkward moments and it is scarcely a consolation that they intrude upon us with a disembodied voice when one is secretly wishing they were disembowelled instead. It is in trying moments, when people make too many demands or make demands at the wrong time, that manners are needed most. Now that my telephone number is known to be in the Manhattan directory, I receive calls all day and all night. Frequently they come at times when I am dashing out of the house, or already asleep. The difficulty with the phone is that nobody can see that you already have your hat on your head and umbrella in hand, so they are free to regard your excuse ('Oh, you've rung me up just as I was leaving') as a lie. A great many people find it hard to believe that you are not ready at every moment to give them your time, your entire attention and your entire energy. So when people ring me up and I *am* leaving the house, I try to give a little explanation of *why* I'm leaving the house, even where I am going. I try to paint a picture of what they cannot see so that they will be more inclined to react considerately and not feel insulted if they receive short shrift. It could be that one is dashing into the washroom, or that one's hair is covered with soap; it could be anything. It may be pure fiction, but by giving a caller a good excuse and a few details of why you cannot talk for long, you will create an impression that placates his feelings while placing a limit on the annoyance to you. You have to take a little extra time – although you may not want to take *any* time speaking to the person in question – in order to save time in ending the unwanted conversation as quickly as possible.

I generally find that most telephone callers dawdle and need polite guidance to get to where they're going, probably because the telephone lends itself to being used as an instrument of informality – and informality is a waste of time. A lot of people repeat what they say. They ask the same question several times, either forgetting that you've already answered it or else forgetting *what* you said when you answered. You must never say, 'I've already answered that question, shall we go on to something else?' You must begin all over again with just as much enthusiasm but never with the same words because when you utter the same words you used the first time they may remember they have asked you the question before, and may even think that by repeating the same words you are *reminding* them of their forgetfulness. Since it is absolutely essential that no one should ever be made to seem boring or repetitious, you must avoid any suggestion that you are weary of what they are saying.

Then there are people whose questions *cannot* be answered and they will not accept your legitimate excuse, 'I don't know – I don't know your mother, so how can I tell whether she is pretending to be ill or not?' You must look or sound as if you will, just by talking, arrive at the answer. Not that you necessarily have the answer, but you are interested in working from the outside in until you have the answer, by saying, 'Describe what your mother does and says when she is trying to prevent you from leaving the house because she says she's too ill for you to leave' – or whatever it is. All of these situations can be trying – fascinating, but trying – but at least they show that people are interested in you, try to make communication with you and place some store, if only temporarily, in what you say. But such people require manipulative skill to prevent their becoming an intolerable nuisance.

Some people, even those with no fame to contend with, feel the need to create a buffer between themselves and the jingling-jangling telephone world. The rich hire secretaries to screen all their calls and then set up appointments for real conversations. Members of the middle class become subscribers to telephone-answering services or else they buy a robot – a little tin man who utters a fixed message and tells callers to chirp when they hear the beep. It has become a craze among the electronic generation to leave 'cute' prerecorded messages on their answering machines (husky woman's voice, 'I'm all tied up right now but as soon as he leaves I'll return your call....') so that even routine calls end up sounding like Dial-a-Joke. The line between defence (having a machine to filter one's calls) and offence (wasting the time of everyone who rings up with a self-indulgent gag) is a fine one. Answering machines can have their uses, but like anything touched by humans, they are more likely to be abused.

All New Yorkers are familiar with the aural equivalent of Chinese water torture encountered nowadays when telephoning a large store or company. Instead of receiving prompt, efficient and courteous service you find yourself listening to Ponchielli's 'Dance of the Hours' or some other musical claptrap while waiting for someone to answer your call. There is probably a theory worked out by some psychologist (who instead of remaining a good doctor went into market research instead) which states that people will wait longer for service if they are soothed by lullabies into comatose submission – while the company saves on the number of workers it hires to answer your calls. As for the poor, the only buffer they can afford is to unplug their phones – with the obvious disadvantage that when the quiz-master calls offering an all-expenses-paid trip to Bermuda in exchange for an explanation of who Maria Montez was, they won't hear about it. But then the poor always have bad luck it seems.

To me a telephone is a window facing the outside world and I feel obliged to keep it open: who am I to refuse a call from anyone? Instead of using a buffer to protect me I employ the art of manners so as to be open to every social opportunity

(I need every free meal I can get) but not to be imposed upon
unbearably by bores, windbags and psychos. One day, I fancy,
someone will ring up, saying, 'I have this friend you may like,
coming into town. She used to be in the movies. Why don't
we all have lunch tomorrow?' And when I show up the next
day, the surprise guest will turn out to be Maureen O'Hara.
She will smile and I will hear an Aeolian harp playing an Irish
air, and our memories will do a little jig. Meanwhile, back on
the Lower East Side: one of my most frequent callers, at
present, is someone I've never met. She has a young-sounding
voice, and introduced herself after *The Naked Civil Servant*
was repeated in the New York area on television. She seems
timid and shy but is not without perceptiveness. 'The thing
that struck me the most when watching the film is that you
never wanted anything for yourself.' I was delighted that she
had noticed something so subtle that even professional critics
had not detected it, yet for the rest of her calls she had
nothing much to say and merely needed someone 'nice' to
share her nothingness with. While I answer all of my
telephone calls with the same words ('Oh, yes ...' with a yard-
long drawl), upon learning that the caller may be a meander-
ing nuisance I spring into action with defensive manners.
'Oh, how nice of you to call, I can spare about five minutes if
you like but then I must dash to the post office. I have this
urgent letter that must go to Europe and I'm trying to catch
the special delivery pick-up at noon. How *are* you...?' For a
maximum of five minutes I am a captive audience drying my
nails, then the guillotine falls. 'Oh my goodness, it's nearly
twelve, I'll barely make it. Yes *so* nice talking to you, too.'
And then I go back to doing whatever I was doing – which
sometimes is as little as staring at a blank wall and admiring
its purity.

Of course I lie to people. But I lie altruistically – for our
mutual good. The lie is the basic building block of good
manners. That may seem mildly shocking to a moralist – but
then what isn't? This book is not for the morally squeamish.
If a moralist were to go into the bed-linen business, instead of
inventing something as exquisite as an eiderdown comforter,
he would probably come up with a *discomforter* filled with
thistles and thorns so that, even in our sleep, we would kick

against the pricks. Morality, even when it is purely humanistic – devoid of all mystical and religious influences – leads ultimately to death. We must give all that we have and all that we are. A moralist, for instance, must always tell the truth; a well-mannered person could hardly survive a single day without telling a few lies and without allowing a good many more to pass unchallenged. Good manners *do* draw the line at a convenient place – but quietly.

Mr Charles Chaplin once told Sophia Loren that she lacked only one laudable attribute – the ability to say 'No'. She seems, in spite of this deficiency, to be doing all right, but if the rest of us, who lack her indestructibility, never evaded any claim upon our time and energy we would rapidly become extinct. The takers of this world are numberless and insatiable.

Once this distinction between morality and manners has been perceived and understood, how to behave well becomes in broad terms self-evident: Give generously what you do not need; withhold quietly what you cannot bear to part with. Praise lavishly anyone who can never constitute a serious rival; disparage subtly those who might outstrip you. What Mr Machiavelli considered to be politically expedient for a prince is socially expedient even for those not of noble blood. He recommended that a prince should do all the harm he felt to be absolutely necessary on one day but should spread good deeds through the year.

Never argue with your wife or husband, nor hit your children, in public; deal with your loathed ones at home. Present a clean appearance both physically and spiritually to neighbours and even to strangers, reserve your nastiness for your family. If the difference between your private and public behaviour is remarked upon, never deny it; make a great show of bearing the rebuke with good grace. Learn to be more accepting of life's vicissitudes: accept opportunities for self-gratification cheerfully; accept compliments without self-deprecation; accept gifts without saying the giver shouldn't have given them; accept money at once ... accept advice and get rid of it immediately, and as the astute Mr Shaw once said, 'Do *not* do unto others what you would have them do unto you: they may not have the same tastes.'

There is a nursery-school of thought which advocates that people should be *sincere*: that they should be constantly expressing what's on their minds. Creeping Sloppiness, the philosophy of the unruly class, holds 'sincerity', 'spontaneity' and 'candour' in great esteem; but in fact the usual results of practising these pseudo-virtues is confusion, misunderstanding and hurt feelings. In my experience most so-called 'truths' are emotional in their base and far more unreliable than a lie. How many times has 'I love you' been whispered in the evening only to turn into 'I can't stand you' by the morning? Truth-telling has an inflated reputation in our culture: every time the word 'truth' is spoken one practically hears a heavenly choir of philosophers and theologians singing the Hallelujah Chorus. Yet if we constantly told people exactly what we felt at any given moment there would be nothing but incivil chaos. A woman boarding a bus would say to the driver, 'Well, it's about time you got here you fat slob.' And he would reply, 'Oh shut up you old bag.' A teenager sitting nearby would exclaim aloud, 'I hope I don't look like you ugly toads when I get older.' And a woman sitting next to him would say, 'Have you had a bath lately?' And so on down the aisle until, goaded and gouged, everyone's adrenalin flows and blood flows after it. Telling 'the truth' is an activity that generally pleases only one person and even then it is likely that the pain of it pleases him. But a well-mannered lie soothes and massages both parties so that the surface of their social relations is as smooth as a glassy sea.

Whenever someone says to me, 'But what do you *really* think about me (him, her, it)?' what I *really* think is that it's time to go. To say what we think to our superiors would be inexpedient; to say what we think to our equals would be ill mannered and to say what we think to an inferior is unkind. Good manners occupy the terrain between fear and pity.

So we aim at being inwardly calm while feigning enthusiasm for others and we come to realize that the difference between 'a truth' and 'a lie' is as inconsequential as the difference between 'non-fiction' and 'fiction': as long as it's 'a good read' and pleases an audience who cares how it may be classified by pedants?

Ideally, our manners should be authentic – that is, one tries to integrate good manners with one's self so that they become one, at which point good manners become an acquired second nature. But this takes time and much experience. At first, behaving well (especially in situations where one is tempted to behave badly) will seem strange and something of a strain, because in an impolite society good manners are a form of irony, and the human brain probably consumes more oxygen and calories when it is being spiritually athletic than when it is merely slouched in a heap watching television. I know these words go against the grain of several modern fashions of thought – and may bring tears to the eyes of those poor souls who are searching the streets for 'a meaningful relationship' and 'in-depth one-on-one communication'. Such notions – the Holy Grails of pop sociology – are on a par with the medieval belief in unicorns and other fabulous creatures, which – as long as the belief endured – many people sought in dark forests and grottoes, and occasionally claimed to find. A basic right of man is the right to be deceived; all I say is that he should be deceived in such a way that he feels comfortable.

With this much understood we can proceed to the next course – Advanced Crisperanto or the technique of honing our words so fine and sharp that we can say what we mean without giving offence even in the most delicate of situations. Manners, remember, are a way of getting what we want without appearing to be an absolute swine. That is why we go to all this trouble of getting along with people, for we never know who it will be handy to know when the next wave of the future sweeps around our feet. To know a great many people, favourably and superficially, is the best security blanket that anyone can have.

5

Advanced Crisperanto

'Manners are of more importance than laws. ...
Manners are what vex or soothe, corrupt or purify,
exalt or debase, barbarize or refine us, by a constant,
steady, uniform, insensible operation, like that of
the air we breathe in.'

Edmund Burke, *Letters on a Regicide Peace*

Some people are born fault-finders: of the whole man they
seek only the Achilles' heel.

The difference between a well-mannered person who
chooses not to react to every human foible he encounters, and
someone who can't keep a bitchy temperament under control, is not that the former is unobservant, but that he has
achieved a certain measure of inner calm. He doesn't feel
compelled to build himself up by tearing others down.

To be constantly on the lookout for real or imaginary
slights by other people, or shortcomings in them, *predisposes*
one to bad manners: even if one resists commenting upon
whatever flaws one spies in others, one is not going to enjoy
the company of people privately regarded as fools.

A well-mannered person does indeed see the gaffes of
others – anyone who makes a concerted effort to become
conscious of the ramifications of his manners is bound to be
conscious of all that goes on around him. But instead of
making others feel bad by making reproving remarks he
discreetly avoids being victimized by their misbehaviour.
Such a manœuvre falls under the heading of 'defensive
manners': you see trouble coming and you cross the street, as
it were, so that you may continue on your way, whistling a
happy tune. By contrast, a person with a bitchy streak is
always on the prowl for sarcastic opportunities, his ego
thriving on the discomfort of others. What makes the fault-

finder so compulsive about uncovering defects in others is that he is striving to reduce everything and everybody to the same level of mediocrity that he accepts for himself. The well-mannered person ardently wants social relations to run smoothly; his actions and words are designed to bring out the best in people. But the perverse fault-finder *doesn't* want people to behave better than he does; most of his words and actions are designed to bring out the worst in people, creating a maximum of confusion and misunderstanding.

The basic measure of defensive manners is: weed your social garden. The world is full of people and there is no reason to endure those who are more trouble than they are worth. Instead of surrounding yourself with tiresome people – be they boors or bores – keep the revolving door revolving.

Nearly all of the people who write in to Miss Manners (in her syndicated column) do so because they wish to complain about someone's rude behaviour and want advice on how to rebuke him. It's a waste of time: don't try to change your guest's behaviour – if they aren't up to scratch, don't ask them back. Life is too short to be spent in a constant struggle separating the good from the bad; there is barely enough time to separate the excellent from the merely good.

Another general rule: cultivate as large a vocabulary as possible: the well-mannered person requires a great store of tactful expressions. We should upgrade our conversational skills in order to increase our *choice* of what to say, so that people will get our meaning without our having to insult them.

Instead of being stuck with calling large people 'fat' we can now say they are 'imposing', or 'Junoesque'. Instead of describing someone as 'skinny' we can say 'slim', 'slender', or 'sylphlike'. This is a common practice on a rudimentary level, for most people maintain two sets of adjectives – an alkaline list for those present, and an acidic list for absentees: those who are absent can be called 'greedy', those at the table have 'hearty appetites'; those absent are 'opinionated'; those present 'know their own minds'; absentees are 'tyrannical', present company are 'born leaders', and so on. Euphemisms have a bad reputation among the young, the wild and the free, and others who delight in knee-capping people with their philosophical hammers, but to say indirectly what you mean so that your message is unmistakable but your delivery gives no offence is one of the most subtle arts that the human mind can devise. Euphemisms are not, as many young people think, useless verbiage for that which can and should be said bluntly; they are like secret agents on a delicate mission, they must airily pass by a stinking mess with barely so much as a nod of the head, make their point of constructive criticism and continue on in calm forbearance. Euphemisms are unpleasant truths wearing diplomatic cologne.

We must not use our vocabularies, however, to make people feel uncomfortable or simply to show that we have spent hours in studying a dictionary (or, in my case, doing crossword puzzles). If I were to use the word 'avaricious' and I sensed that the person I was talking to was not familiar with the word I might add 'greedy about money' as if I were amplifying my own thoughts rather than explaining the word to him. Although one tries to address the world with as much intelligence and finesse as possible, one tries to eliminate any trace of condescension in one's speech.

There are other preventive measures which can be employed to minimize the inconsideration of others. For example, it is prudent to inform guests beforehand of the hour at which you expect a party to end ('I'm having a dinner on Sunday between seven and ten and would love to see you . . .') so that straggling is discouraged. If anyone does linger and their loitering is not an agreeable prospect, this advance warning allows you to say, around ten-fifteen, 'Oh, it's getting rather late . . . we must get together again some time.' The best way to head off misunderstandings with your guests is to be clear with them ahead of time. Call it 'mirth control' if you like – but the good times of others should not add up to a bad time for the host.

Another means of practising defensive manners is to put the telephone to a rare good use, rather than issue written invitations, for all but the most formal occasions. This allows one to monitor the latest developments in delicate personal situations. One frequently hears nowadays that invited guests fail to respond to party invitations but nevertheless turn up at the last minute, or fail to show at all. The use of the telephone is a preventive measure against the possible bad manners of others who apparently are unaware that by failing to respond to an RSVP they are inconveniencing the host(ess) who then doesn't know how many guests to plan for. The other advantage to a direct invitation by telephone is that it permits one to determine who will be accompanied by whom, if indeed he or she will be accompanied at all. If you have one guest coming whose presence may disconcert another, the telephone conversation allows one to clarify this, and if the discomfiture would be acute, other arrangements may be made ('another time perhaps ... when Mrs Thatcher isn't coming'). A successful host(ess) foresees every conceivable problem and seeks to diffuse any threat to placidity: the perfect social gathering is one that, while gaily animated, generates no visible trace of drunkenness, rancour, illness, lechery or imbecility.

One does not invite rivals – let alone enemies – to the same social function and then hope for the best. Manners are not morals and we cannot use social functions to express approval or disapproval of anyone's private life nor to attempt to solve problems of society. The perfect host(ess) employs manners as a neutral technique of making everyone invited into his or her home *feel* at home, or everyone he or she socializes with in the outer world feel comfortable. Should we feel compelled to work for social change of some sort there are other arenas for appropriate action. Where a host-(ess) is faced with confronting sharply divisive people, he or she should offer different parties. It is a waste of one's resources of hospitality to mix the wrong people on any social occasion as if hoping, or dreaming, that one's home will become a sociological melting pot in which proximity will overcome vast differences in education, taste and aspiration. The most pleasing and successful parties that I have attended were those which *appeared* to be joyously spontaneous, but which in fact had been meticulously planned (as to who was invited, what was served) and imaginatively executed.

Much of what constitutes the 'mild errors' of manners among certain people is based on the assumption – never baldly stated – that somehow he or she is 'special' and thus beyond the rules. For instance, you get someone on the

telephone saying 'Hi, howya doin'?' without identifying who
he is because he *expects* to be recognized, and who when
asked for his identity may even say, 'Well, who do you think
it is?' This is coy and absurd; such informalities are simply
inefficiencies and should be treated as such.

Graver errors that are common in the eighteen-to-thirty
group include open or surreptitious drug use at social gatherings. Most drugs are anti-social in their effects (ultimately, if
not immediately), which is why their use is almost invariably
a breach of manners, but what's worse, most 'recreational
drugs' are illegal and anyone who commits an illegal act on
the premises of a host(ess) is involving others in a criminal
offence. Whatever defence a person may believe exists for the
use of certain drugs (such as marijuana), a social gathering,
hosted by another, is no occasion for breaking the law and
flaunting it. Parties are not the place for advancing social
reforms of *any* kind. If one is hell-bent on using illegal drugs
it is best to ingest them on one's own premises, and so not
involve others. Since most people cannot tell the difference
between natural and chemically induced stupidity you are
likely to pass yourself off as a dull but happy fellow. Anyone
who lives in sin in the eyes of society – be it for the use of
drugs or illegal forms of sexuality – should have the decency
to 'cool it' when in the presence of real people (i.e. those who
form the majority of a society and establish its standards).

As to the use of other drugs – tobacco or alcohol – these can
be discouraged assuming the host(ess) so wishes by a variety
of means. It is possible for a host(ess) to say or have printed on
an invitation, 'This is not a smoking household.' One does
this only if cigarette smoke is considered a sufficient irritant
(or health hazard) to justify the faintly pompous policy.
Again, it is best to state this clearly, before the guest has
arrived for the choice must be his: 'Do I want to go to Mr
Clean-Air's dinner party and not smoke for several hours?' If
the small persistent voice of his tobacco habit says, '(cough,
cough) What a damnable inconvenience! Well I just won't go
...' then at least he won't feel hurt for not being invited. It is
bad manners for a guest to say, 'Have you got an ashtray?' as if
permission to smoke is taken for granted. Allowing a smoker
to smoke may well irritate others, but forbidding him to

smoke irritates only himself.

As for alcohol: the best way to ward off 'problem drinkers' is not to give cocktail parties, and not to encourage the sort of occasion where drinking gets out of hand. You can serve wine only in an attempt to keep some of your guests sober longer than they would be if spirits were available or you can concentrate on giving brunches or dinners where alcohol consumption is usually more moderate. You can invite guests in for a 'midnite snack' after some form of entertainment (in addition to limiting your guests' alcohol usage, this stratagem is an economical way of being gracious). If all these tactics fail, and you've still got a drunk on your hands, more serious measures are in order. Perhaps you will have to weed your social garden again.

The problems that one encounters on an occasional basis in hosting a soirée are nothing compared to the domestic discords that can occur when two or more people are sharing a residence. Even at the most gloomy party one can console oneself by saying, 'This too shall pass,' and be reasonably sure it *will* end before sunrise, when all the vampires creep back into their crypts. But with spouses, in-laws, flatmates (and all those who the more disruptive of your life their behaviour becomes the more often they tell you they love you – what kind of excuse is that?), it is no easy matter to extricate oneself from a trying situation. I do not allow this problem to arise in my own life; I have not lived with anyone since reaching my mid-thirties, and have not had the remotest wish to be seen by someone else eating my morning corn-beef hash and eggs, with a scraggly beard and my hair in curlers. I would rather move to the Third World and be crushingly poor and alone in a rice paddy than be pent up in a penthouse with some professional cell-mate who insists on being my soul-mate. I don't want to sing 'The Nearness of You' to anyone; but judging from the expanding list of 'Shared Accommodation' classifieds in the papers the bulk of humanity is lining up, for reasons of economics or debauchery, to live in communal beehives where the days are filled with a socializing buzz and the nights are rendered sleepless by snoring and other nocturnal emissions.

For those who don't have enough cents to live alone a few

guidelines from the sidelines may help: clarity of communication coupled with tact is an invaluable tool in preventing misunderstandings from occurring in any social situation, but it is crucial when two or more people share a dwelling together. Flatmates can help preserve a sense of privacy (and 'breathing space') by informing one another on a regular basis what their schedule is likely to be, so that when one is staying in, the other may plan to go out. That way their residence is used with maximum efficiency. Clear, consistent arrangements about the occasional sharing of food and supplies are also helpful; one tries wherever possible to reduce the everyday domestic details to a dependable formula, considerate to all, agreed upon by all, and requiring little further discussion. This may seem elementary, but in my experience, which comes largely from observing the mistakes of others, many people find it difficult to share in the running of a peaceable kingdom. No sooner has one individual agreed (in apparently sound mind and good spirits) to perform a certain function for the well-being of the household, than he wants to change it. By the third week or so, he forgets the function altogether, and by the fourth is complaining about 'being taken for granted'. So you are back to square one again, trying to define who will do what and when. The younger your flatmates are the sloppier they are likely to be; the older they are the more eccentric and brittle they are likely to be. Without people, our lives may seem to be an arid waste, but with them, the desert suddenly becomes a minefield. The man or woman who is an amusing delight to meet once a month for a meal and a movie may turn out to be an irascible neurotic with a drinking problem upon moving in: few people look their best in extreme close-up.

Matters can get worse: if your flatmate brings home guests you may well find that in addition to having less privacy you also end up having less of everything else: food, liquor, soap, shampoo, anything that is not locked up. It is, of course, the responsibility of a house-mate to give his guests a towel and facecloth (so that they won't use yours), and to point out to them what shelves in the medicine cabinet hold your property, and so on. But if you get stuck sharing with someone of extreme casualness, and then, even worse, hit with their guests whose manners are non-existent, everything you own will be subject to erosion and petty larceny. Since you are presumably sharing a place for economic reasons, this slow, steady eroding of whatever you buy will be a constant irritation, for every glass of juice, every inch of toothpaste is a further pinch in your own tight budget.

With reasonable people, remedial action is never far from hand but what makes cohabitation so problematic is that most people are not reasonable: they are far more likely to see your faults than their own. This tendency is aggravated if by further mischance the place you are sharing belongs to them. If two people take an apartment together, they may later decide that they are not getting on and bring the arrangement to an end, but at least they will be obliged to treat one another as equals and they are likely to try to make their domestic arrangement work.

If the place you are sharing, however, is the property of the other person, you are likely to be regarded – in stressful moments – as an interloper with minimal rights, and are likely to be treated arbitrarily in any disagreement.

In the early stages of sharing accommodation, you can try to solve your problems through discussion; beyond that, you must employ defensive manners – and begin avoiding your flatmate as much as possible and protecting your property from the petty pilferage of his guests. This policy is only a stop-gap measure, for it is likely to cost more than you planned or can afford to eat your meals out or go away for weekends in order to preserve your sanity. As these extra costs mount, the whole point of sharing a place to save money will become blunted and worn down to pointlessness. Thus, exhausted and exasperated, you will have to begin again, looking for a place to lay your weary head – alone.

Man is basically a modest animal who sometimes behaves immodestly. The current era is a period of such derangement. All bodily functions are unpleasant and, for the most part, we are aware of this. By mutual consent and in compliance with the law, most physical functions are performed out of sight of others. Due to the modern trend, however, of people becoming regressively infantile in the name of being progressively uninhibited, we are likely to be exposed to all sorts of tasteless behaviour that aspires to being Rabelaisian but which, in fact, is merely revolting. Things were better when couples didn't mistake the living room for a bedroom in full view of everyone else. Physical passion should never be given a physical expression in public – any more than vomiting or defecating. No one, thank goodness, advocates that people should go about with long green strands of snot dangling from their noses in the name of nasal freedom, yet quite a few people have been converted in recent years to a belief that it is permissible for them to inflict the sights, sounds and smells of their bodies on any innocent bystander in the name of 'sexual freedom'.

Only a minimum of politeness is required when you live with someone with whom you are in basic agreement. Something more is needed for those to whose opinions and actions you find yourself opposed and, when you find you have settled in with someone thoroughly incompatible, you must avail yourself of all the courtesy of which your vocabulary is capable. The well of togetherness contains a multitude of microparasites that you will never find in the well of loneliness.

If one is constantly frustrated and defeated by the social environment in which one lives, good manners will remain an abstract subject rather than an embodied idea. John Keats once wrote: 'That which is creative must first create itself.' So it is with manners – we must first of all seek out those people and situations most conducive to bringing out the best in us. Then, when we have become calm and strong in our manners, we can take our models of behaviour out into the wider, ruder world, for an airing, a challenge, even an occasional beating. Time and again, throughout our lives, we will follow this tidal pattern of renewal and return – for always the object is to encourage good manners in others through example (rather than through censorious nagging) and when wearied of that tiresome process, to recuperate alone in pleasant surroundings.

6

The World of Sex

'Of all the animals on earth, none is so brutish as
man when he seeks the delirium of coition.'
Edward Dahlberg, *The Edward Dahlberg Reader*

For six sizzling summer weeks during 1983, when most
sensible New Yorkers had departed for breezy beaches or
more temperate climes, an intrepid producer in search of
miraculous profits or a tax loss (which my spies in the world
of high finance tell me is often the same thing – no wonder
the economy is shaky) staged a revival of my one-man show,
entitled: *How to Make It in the Big Time*. Much to my
amazement, hundreds of people showed up each week at the
Actor's Playhouse on Seventh Avenue – such is the drawing
power of air conditioning. Reuters News Service, in an article
about the show, dubbed me 'the powdered Messiah' which
like most journalism adds false excitement to the facts. Even
with my name in lights and my countenance plastered
around New York on posters (now peeling – how fleeting is
fame) I remain the same: Your Humble Savant.

I agreed to be lured out of retirement but only as a stand-in
for Gloria Swanson who was permanently indisposed. I
viewed the show as *my* glorious swan song and wanted to call
it: 'Crisp's Last Stand'. Much of the programme, as in the
past, consisted of questions-and-answers; some of the in-
quiries I received were trivial and begged to be sent up: 'What
sign are you?'

'I'm Septuagenarian.'

The more interesting questions contributed to the field-
work for this book – finding out what situations bother
people the most and determining whether a Crisp manner
could be of any help. Unsurprisingly it was sexual relations –
in the broadest sense – that many people reported as being

difficult to handle, for when men and women stepped outside
traditional roles they became uneasy.

'What does one do about The Pounce?' one woman asked. I
tilted a neatly pencilled eyebrow in surprise. The Pounce is
what lecherous Robert Lovelace kept springing on poor
Clarissa Harlowe. I thought The Pounce went out with 'cads'
and 'bounders'. As someone who no longer wrestles with the
winking Cyclops-of-sex, or need worry about things going
hump in the night, my life is now one long sigh of relief. But
even if I dwell placidly on a platonic plain, it appears my
fellow creatures have their britches full of itches. The woman
explained to me and the rest of the audience that she had had
a terrible experience recently. Like many modern women she
had taken a course in self-defence but then, rather like a
government overarmed with nuclear weapons but deficient in
less apocalyptic weaponry, she found herself in a situation
where all-out kung-fu was clearly not the correct response,
and yet stern measures of some kind were needed. 'What you
want to know,' I interjected, 'is whether there is a polite
alternative to a slap on the face.'

She described the problem: she had come to know, quite
casually and effortlessly, a gentleman who was in his
eighties, or seemed to be. She assumed that this would set her
free of everything but a quiet twilight relationship, so when
he took her out to dinner, and invited her back to his place,
she said 'That would be nice. ...' with lowered guard.

She did not suspect that while her date may have been in
his sunset years this particular sunset was streaked with red
rivulets of lust. No sooner did he get her into his lair than he
pounced – and the evening ended in an undignified physical
struggle. The woman, well-preserved and handsome, looked
as if she could easily have knocked old satyr into the
intensive ward and nine months of Medicare. 'I was trying to
get free,' she said, 'but I didn't want to break any of his brittle
old bones.'

Other women (and one man) testified that they also find
The Pounce a pressing problem, and that its incidence is
increasing. 'It isn't just men who are sexually predatory,' one
wan lad complained. 'You scarcely say "hello" to a woman
these days and she replies, "Your place or mine?"'

'Manners,' I tell them, employing the labour-saving device of self-quotation, 'are a means of getting what we want without appearing to be absolute swine. This means that manners, as I define them, are largely a way of saying "no" to the demands of other people while still being considerate of their feelings. The reason we say "no" is because we want to, or have to; the reason we say "no" *sweetly* is because we have no wish to injure or alienate other people, some of whom we may want to receive assistance or cooperation from in the future.'

Rudeness is also a way of trying to get what you want, and in the short run it may work; you abruptly cut in front of another car during rush hour and sure enough you make it to the next red light two seconds ahead of the pack. Congratulations. But rudeness fails as a general policy because a world where everyone feels free to smash and grab, hack and stab, and shout insults is one that is riddled with malfunctions and aggravations.

Sex is trickier than most situations we have to deal with because people attach so much importance to being 'attractive' or at least 'acceptable'. If a man tries to press you into playing a game of chess and you refuse, it is unlikely that he will be plunged into depression, try to take his own life – or yours – or rush off crying to a therapist. A refusal, however, to pop into bed with him can turn him into a wild beast or a nervous wreck. Saying 'no' to a woman is even more difficult, for hell hath no fury like a woman looking for a new lover. A woman can make a man feel like an oversexed ape if he tries anything, or an emasculated oaf if he doesn't; small wonder there is so much seething misunderstanding between the sexes.

First I wish to make clear, if it is not already well known, that I am an expert on sex by virtue of my inexperience. I have never regarded sex with the slightest awe or reverence. Of course I have done most of the things that can be done with the male plumbing system, but my expertise, such as it is, is based on penetrating insights rather than by penetrating orifices. It is useless to categorize my views as 'liberal' or 'conservative', as I do not funnel my observations through an ideology; besides, like all unfettered human beings, I call no pigeonhole home.

Ever since *The Naked Civil Servant* first appeared I have been interviewed periodically for my views on sex. Most of these interviewers seem to hope that I will say something outrageous – but I am not Oscar Wilde. I simply dive into the straits of confusion and head straight for the white cliffs of the obvious. I have said: 'sex is a mistake', and 'sex is the last refuge of the miserable', and then the interviewers go back to their editors clucking that I am an anti-sexual reactionary. This is especially true when my views have been solicited for 'gay' publications. It has been an article of faith among many homosexuals for the past ten years that the more partners one had in the shortest span of time the more 'liberated' one was held to be.

But now that a modern-day Adam would wear a figleaf not for modesty but to conceal his pustules, and homosexuals are dropping like flies from AIDS, my views on human sexuality seem less anachronistic. I maintain that now that sex is valueless, through repeated depreciations, it is pursued with even greater frenzy; people are doing it more and enjoying it less. If a man has forty orgasms a week what can he expect but death on Sunday? Too much ice-cream, too much salt, too much of anything can make you ill.

Instant sex is a time- and labour-saving device but; as leisure and energy are what we now have to excess, this is no recommendation. For flavour, it will never supersede the stuff you had to peel and cook. This is one of the unpleasant truths that the permissive society has brought to light. We are all now dangerously aware that sexual intercourse is a bit of a bore. What kept the 'divine woman' lark going for so many centuries was romance not the G spot. Of modern woman we are forced to admit that custom can stale her infinite availability.

To replace romance we are now offered every possible kind of kinkiness. It is not a satisfactory substitute. What is wrong with pornography is that it is a successful attempt to sell sex for more than it is worth. I have before me an advertisement for an illustrated book entitled *Women and Their Pets*. The caption reads: 'See the effect that young, ripe and ready women have on this wild collection of turtles, snakes, cats and even Great Danes and you will have seen it all! Truly a giant step into a forbidden world where there are no rules!' This book, full of 'color photos of princesses and their pets', $9.95 plus postage, is not offered in some furtively circulated sleaze rag but in a mainstream mass-circulation magazine, *Playgirl*. Other pages offer feathery doodaws to 'tickle a lady's fancy' or grotesque rubber instruments that look like leftover tools from the Spanish Inquisition. I don't as a rule have anything kind to say about dumb animals but I'm sure it isn't the turtles or the Great Danes that are dashing off to write for the publication, charge card in claw or paw, in order to ogle naked humans.

There is even a device (same issue, same magazine) that looks like a stubby cylinder of soft plastic with a hole in it, the name of which ('Real Pussy') is a brazen lie: 'It vibrates, strokes, gets wet and it even squeezes you when you come! Your money back ($39.95 plus tax) if you can tell it from the real thing in the dark!' We can now trace the trajectory of the sexual revolution: it begins with a group of academic liberals extravagantly defending a mediocre novel by Mr D. H. Lawrence in a court of law employing hifalutin speeches about literary, political and sexual freedom – and it ends in popularizing carnal vulgarity: Hands Solo and his space-age piece of pulsating plastic tail. After I had described this sexual merchandise one night to the audience, one young woman stood up and said, 'It's my impression that most men would be perfectly satisfied, and better off, with a portable vagina. It certainly would be better for them to use a machine than try to turn a woman into something silent and mechanical.' The air was charged with ions and eons of rage.

The war between the sexes is the only one in which both sides regularly sleep with the enemy. For this reason (that no matter what complaints men may have against women, or women against men, they are likely to reach a tense truce by bedtime), one cannot rely on the gunboat diplomacy of feminists in affairs of the heart. Something much more subtle is needed: I recommend Crisperanto as a means of preserving grace and saving face.

First we must address the issue of seduction (of which The Pounce is an abruptly truncated form); we must ask what constitutes good manners for a seducer, and what constitutes good manners for a seducee (willing or unwilling). From an aggressor's point of view, this means how may one invite without coercion? From a victim's point of view, this means how may one refuse without abuse?

It is true, alas, that we live in an age where no one can be trusted to behave themselves where sex is concerned. When I was young, a common defence against seductiveness was to pretend that you hadn't heard or understood remarks which were supposed to lead to a sexual encounter – and that was nearly always accepted. You went on blithely talking about something else. But nowadays it is much more difficult to pretend to be innocent, for lasciviousness is ubiquitously advertised: we have dehumanized sex, and then sexualized everything else – from airline travel to soft drinks. The stance of preserving one's virtue by being obtuse no longer works in today's climate of unrestraint, for the chances are your prospective seducer, far from being shy and nervous and willing to take no response to mean 'no', will turn out to be a sexual evangelist, clutching a copy of *The Playboy Philosophy* under his free arm. If you don't appear to hear his lewd suggestions he will be only too happy to repeat them and if you don't seem to understand he will proceed to explain them, for the sexual evangelist believes he has a god-given *right* to your body and must 'save' you from your inexperience, naïveté, or lack of interest, so that you too will become a convert to life's Passion Play.

If you do not mind throwing all caution to the winds and yourself to the wolves, then reading these comments is a waste of time. All that one can ask is that you clean up afterwards. If, however, you wish to honour a personal code of who you are – no matter what outer society, be it puritanical or libertarian, coerces you into believing you *ought* to be doing and feeling – then ways must be found to preserve your privacy, modesty and individuality without causing a great war between you and the others. Defensive manners are again the key to survival; you must anticipate an invitation to seduction and (if you don't wish to accept) head if off at the pass. In short you must prune the tree of his ardour before it becomes a burning bush.

When someone invites you out to dinner, for example, you must be aware, without the knowledge making you cynical, that no man, woman or child is absolutely safe these days from the long arm and itchy fingers of human lust. It is essential to find out as quickly as possible what someone expects from a relationship before you start to deal with it. It is always disturbing to have to make the transition from wining and dining, dancing and laughing, to suddenly having to say, 'Don't do that!'

It's much harder for women, or rather it was harder for women to convey a refusal which the man believes, because in the days when they were still ... women, as opposed to people, a man *expected* a woman to resist. He expected to have to wheedle and nag to get past her defences; it was certainly not generally assumed that when a woman said 'no' that she meant 'no' and as a result both sexes moved towards rape because rape was the only way that a man could get what he wanted. In fact, a man didn't actually know when he was raping a woman or not, because she *must* say 'no' (only whores said 'yes'), and therefore he made fiercer and fiercer advances until she gave way. Even then she would maintain to the last ditch – and beyond – the idea that she was an unwilling victim of his appetites. Due to this history of coyness, women have a credibility problem when it comes to refusing sex, and men have a mythological problem in that they see themselves as having to conquer a woman, cross-pollinating their 'roughness' with her 'refinement'. Even today, it is usual for the man to make the first suggestion that their relationship be sexual, the woman merely responds. My advice to any woman who wishes to avoid The Pounce – that she must try to convey that the answer is 'no' before the question is even asked – requires consummate tact for she doesn't want to annoy the gentleman who is taking her out by having him think: well, you're taking yourself for granted, rather. I'm only inviting you out for tea damnit! In short: you don't want to be in the *other* awkward position of refusing a proposal that you were never going to get: it only draws attention to your vanity, and that you consider yourself a most pounce-worthy object.

So we cannot say, 'I'd love to have dinner with you on

Friday, Roger, but I don't want any funny business afterwards,' because that is presumptuous, and gratuitously tactless. If one does not know Roger well, and wishes merely to
'test the waters', the same aim – of going to dinner but
limiting one's availability – could be politely accomplished
by saying, 'I'd love to have dinner with you, Roger, but I'm
afraid I have to be back home (or somewhere else) by such-
and-such a time, for such-and-such a reason.' If Roger is
harbouring darker designs for the evening, he may then say,
'Oh another time perhaps.' But if he still insists that meeting
for dinner is what he wants ('Well, both of us have to eat some
time that evening don't we? Might as well get together') then
you are in the clear. You have put protective borders on the
situation and the chance of anything unpleasant happening
has been reduced.

Most dinner engagements (as in the case of the middle-aged
woman and her older gentleman cited earlier) are complicated
by the fact that one person pays (usually the man) and a
woman then feels compromised when Count Dracula leans
over to kiss her: he has, perhaps, picked her up in his car,
driven her to some romantic candlelit restaurant, bought her
a lovely meal, entertained her agreeably – and then, he
pounces. He isn't saying baldly that he thinks she can be had
for the price of a meal, but he probably expects it to be a
mitigating factor, should she waver in granting her favours.
To get around this, a woman who is going out with an
unknown quantity, should build herself a hedge against
seduction. 'How nice of you to invite me ... I'd love to go,
Jeffrey. I would like to pay my own way if you don't mind ...'
In accepting an invitation to dine but weaving into the reply
her intention to pay for herself she will at least be demonstrating her independence. Even if he says, 'No, No, I *want* to
take you out ...' he has got part of the message. If one wants
to send a stronger signal, one could say, 'I'd love to go to
dinner with you, Jeffrey, but it always embarrasses me to be
in anyone's debt ...' then if he says, 'Well I wouldn't consider
you to be in my debt merely because I bought you a dinner,'
then she's in the clear. He knows he mustn't go back on his
word, and if he does pounce, your prearrangements make it
less insufferable to say, 'I thought we'd gone into all that.'

What I am saying – contrary to tradition – is that it must be the woman who sets the terms of a relationship, and she must do this very early, without actually raising the issue of a man's intentions.

This may be done through fables or parables. She may pass along some dreadful story of a man who pounced, and then say, 'I do so like being with you, Bob, because you never force yourself on me. Whereas some of my other friends are nothing but problems.' Having been commended for being a gentleman, Sir Robert is bound to behave gallantly. He may not call again ... but at least you have avoided an emotional mess and a hideous physical struggle.

By sending a number of clear signals, early in the evening, or better still before the date has ever taken place, that indicate what the terms of the meeting are to be, a woman (or a man – if *he* expects to be the object of someone's passionate pursuit) can greatly reduce the number and severity of misunderstandings between the sexes. If asked by her date, 'Shall I see you home?' a woman can reply, 'How kind of you to offer, but I'd hate to trouble you going all that way because I won't be able to invite you in ...' for some reason. Anything will do, as long as she makes this clear, *before* they have departed for her home, *not* on her doorstep, so that the man is forewarned and is free to make a choice.

There is a beautiful moment in a wonderful movie, *Queen of the Stardust Ballroom*, in which two middle-aged people (portrayed by Maureen Stapleton and Vincent Gardenia) reach the awkward moment of saying goodnight after their first date. She says, 'Well, it's been a lovely evening. I've enjoyed myself enormously, but I have to get up early.' And he says, 'Oh, please let me stay a little longer.' And she replies, 'I'm really not ready for that sort of thing.' He has carefully not said, 'Let's pop into bed,' and she has tactfully not said 'no'. Their exchange is clearly understood. The words she uses are inspiredly correct; had she said, 'I'm not the kind of person who likes to get quickly involved' (which may sound like a very slight variation), she would be implying, 'You are just a beast who would pop into bed with anyone but don't imagine that I have sunk as low as you.' In refusing a sexual invitation, one should never take the high road of self-righteousness. Manners demand that we appear to be less than others. 'I may be very old fashioned. ...' is always a good line to use. One practically apologizes for having to say 'no'. You must somehow convey that your approach to sex does not permit casual encounters whilst not reproving your friend for his laid-back laxities. Needless to say, one never resorts to the low blows of casting aspersions upon your friend's physical appearance, or his lack of desirability in your eyes. The whole point to taking a serious interest in manners is that we want to find ways of preserving our self-respect *and* the self-respect of others. A line like, *'Me?* Go to bed with *you?* Are you kidding?' is as ill mannered as The Pounce itself.

One should never introduce a sexual element into a relationship if none is intended; if you do, and it works, you cannot claim to be surprised if someone tries to seduce you. It is ill mannered to flirt (to promise that which will never be given), and doubly so if you are dressed suggestively (don't try to say that you had no idea that your scantily clad body might be of interest to the TV repairman). There are even situations where it is ill mannered to resist seduction. If you have misled someone into thinking that you are available and made frequent allusions to the subject of sex in your manner, dress and speech, if you have accepted hospitality and other gifts and shown no concern where such generosity might lead, then instead of struggling and protesting when The Pounce comes, you should acknowledge your responsibility and accept the consequences. In most cases an act of unwelcome sex is no more bother than being vaccinated, so there's no point going on about it as if it were the fate worse than death. With skill and good manners you can avoid having to make this sacrifice, but should you find yourself in a compromising situation largely of your own making, you should stop defending your virtue and start worrying about your maturity. It will give you something to think about while the savage pumper bangs away.

As to the poor beleaguered seducer – what of him? (Or her, now that women are joining the army.) Can we doctor his bedside manners? No one who is truly well mannered will attempt to seduce a woman at their first meeting. Ideally a gentleman would expect to put up with two or three sexless encounters before saying, 'Would you like to come back to my place?'

However feeble the excuse that may be given for saying 'no', a gentleman always accepts it. If a woman says, 'I can't invite you in, the place is too untidy,' he does not say, 'Oh I love untidiness,' because he ought to know damn well what she means. A gentleman doesn't pounce ... he glides. If a woman sits on a piece of furniture which permits your sitting beside her, you are free to regard this as an invitation, though not an unequivocal one. If she sits in a chair, you are not really free to sit on the arm; the words, 'Surely you would be more comfortable over there,' mean 'Go away,' although whether they mean go away for ever or only go away for the time being you will have to work out later.

The Pounce is desperate; The Glide is calm. The Pounce is clumsy with frustration; The Glide is airborne with sang-froid. You sit next to a woman, you put your arm along the back of the couch, you compliment her in some physical way (saying how nice she looks this evening). If she moves away, you've had it; if she doesn't move at all, you can pursue the matter a little further; if by chance she moves a bit closer to you, you can break out into a smile (inside). When you have actually kissed her and she has not squeaked, run away or hit you, you may assume that you can proceed further but with caution. A man should treat a woman's feelings with all the acute respect he would have for nature when shooting the rapids in a wild river. You proceed tentatively in Braille with your seduction, the less said the better. You should have all the tools of your trade discreetly handy – only in Woody Allen movies is it amusing for a man aspiring to be a woman's lover to be running around in boxer shorts trying to find a contraceptive.

Later, when the beast-with-two-backs has finished its lowly task and reverted to its separate selves, and the woman is musing over the mystery of life and you are contemplating the meaninglessness of existence, whilst the two of you are sharing a post-coital cigarette (or, if non-smokers, a post-sexual mint) in an effort to boost your blood-sugar levels after so much anxiety and strain, as you lie exhausted from the ritual of compulsive excitation and hollow release, you may well wonder if it was all worth it. Even if your mind in a lucid interval is sceptical about the current market value of sex, your body will be clamorous for a new round of sensation within twenty-four hours, and the whole cycle will begin again. Practically every human life consists of a collision between sexual determinism and free will; the life of our bodies keeps us earthbound. There is little dignity to be found here but there can be this much saving grace: it hardly ever happens that two people want one another equally and simultaneously, men and women are always at sixes-and-sevens in their moods and desires. This frequently means that sex is a hostile act – one person gets his way, the other merely complies. Indeed one could say as a general rule: men get laid but women get screwed. Once you perceive sex in this light – that it is not some gift of love you are magnanimously bestowing upon another but basically a selfish desire of your own that you want gratified – you will be obliged to recognize that your lady-friend or gentleman-friend is not part of you (even if they agree to share part of life's journey with you) and are certainly not your possession. You have no 'right' to their bodies – or anything else. You may only take that which is freely given through diplomatic relations.

An imperfect gentleman, which is the most that a modern man can aspire to be, as he – and we – have obviously compromised with the rules of decorum that were upheld in earlier times, at least has the morning-after consolation of knowing that he treated a woman like a lady, which may be better than she deserved but which was no less that what his code of self-respect demanded. When a man (or woman) is mature enough to realize that there are rewards and satisfactions beyond the brute urgency of orgasms, and the highest satisfaction of all is knowing that you have done your best to treat people well, no matter how they have treated you, then a simple disappointment like 'striking out' in an attempted seduction will no longer seem of much consequence. Besides, when the problem of sex rears its head there's always a solution at hand. One should never be dependent on others for the *quantity* of your orgasms – nor the quality for that matter.

When you reach my age, of course, sitting in front of a metaphorical fireplace in calm reflection of the slapstick tragedy of human life, even the story of *Othello* seems comic. All that fuss over a handkerchief. And a woman. Needless to say, it is always bad manners to murder the one you profess to love.

We have barely scratched the soft skin of this subject, for I have dealt only with how a man or woman might better behave than they commonly do the first time that the subject of sex arises. Now we will consider how manners may help in the longer stretch of an affair or intimate friendship. Any fool knows how to make love troublesome; I propose to show, through the use of good manners, love made easier.

7

Love Made Easy

'Manners are the happy way of doing things.'
Ralph Waldo Emerson, *The Conduct of Life*

'What may be done with a man whom you have allowed to make love to you only to realize that you never want to say "yes" again?' a woman plaintively asked me one evening.

'It often happens that when we think we're making whoopee we're only making a *whoops!* instead,' I replied. 'Saying "no" to someone who has already rummaged through our drawers is tricky, but take heart – even Rome, once sacked, did not have to be sacked again and again.'

The difficulty with saying 'no' to someone to whom we have already said 'yes' is that he is bound to think there was something unsatisfactory about the first sexual encounter. Having already lost our immortal soul, something more than a simple 'no' is required in situations where we are badly compromised. We must conduct ourselves as if the world were a more spiritual place than it actually is. We must be painstakingly considerate of others – especially those whom we must disappoint.

When one accepts another date with a man (or a woman) who has every reason to believe that we are already conquered, one cannot feign surprise when he or she makes a move to wrap up the evening in physical congress. Once you have let down your guard and allowed strangers to cross your moat you are bound to find it a hassle to get them out of your castle. A second date with a conquering hero will undoubtedly be interpreted as a sequel to the first, perhaps even the beginning of a long-running serial in which one will be expected to 'break a lance' with the horny knight whenever he's inclined to joust. Saying 'no' to a man bulging with expectations is never easy, but saying 'no' to a man who has

74

cast us in the feature role of his X-rated dreams (note who gets to be writer and director) requires consummate tact to prevent a tactless consummation.

You *cannot* say or imply that the sexual encounter which you allowed to take place on an earlier occasion was a mistake, or a waste of time and that you don't intend to go through the bother again. You must find an excuse for saying 'no' that does not cast even a thin shadow of derision upon his human frailties. You can plead temporary insanity ('I don't know what came over me, I can't think what I was doing . . .') or you can drag in your conscience to play one of its occasional roles ('I realize that what we did was wrong, the fault is entirely mine – such an incident must not occur again'). You should be aware, however, in having to make these excuses, that you have passed from the stage of birth control to that of abortion, for in saying 'yes', even once, to a man, you have planted a seed in his mind that his actions are acceptable to you, perhaps even desired by you, and now you are frustrating those hopes. While bringing a man's illusions to an end at an early stage is ultimately kinder than allowing them to grow into some monstrous misunderstanding, the responsibility for terminating his expectations is not to be shrugged off. The abuse you heap upon yourself is well deserved.

When you have had a prolonged affair with someone and wish to terminate it, you're in real trouble. In my own life I always waited patiently for unwanted guests to leave – even the kind who stayed for several years. It is better to let others tire of you than to be the one who is first to leave, but in situations where one feels compelled to sever a relationship I recommend withdrawal, evasion and silence rather than the vicious battles that people often end up having when they try to 'explain' why they are leaving or why they believe a certain relationship has 'failed'. Such explanations are usually hurtful, not helpful, which is why they are to be avoided. The truth is, most relationships are so ill considered and ill conceived that there are no better reasons for ending the arrangements than there were for starting them in the first place, and anything one has to say about the subject of 'what went wrong' will turn out to be poppycock. It is better to close a door quietly, leave quickly, and keep your mouth shut than to engage in an orgy of accusation over who-owes-what-to-whom. There is probably no polite way of ending an affair except by constantly putting obstacles in the way of any further meetings between your unstable self and the man foolish enough to believe that he loves you. A man should take three consecutive refusals to meet him as a definite sign that an affair is over. He should not pursue the matter beyond this – even if he's a Romantic poet, whereas once he would have pursued the matter for a maladjusted lifetime. As a general rule in our modern times a man must accept that when the cock cries thrice and is thrice denied it is time to take his erection elsewhere.

We live in an era when there is little consensus about anything and virtually no conception about what constitutes good behaviour in any relationship where 'love' is concerned, so even if we behave in an exemplary manner towards others it does not follow that they will abide by the same policies of *politesse*. In today's climate of aggressive self-indulgence we can expect to be woken up at three-in-the-morning by some former flatmate/lover, pounding his fists and stomping his feet in a rage, and demanding that we turn our mediocre domestic drama into the stuff of Grand Opera – without, alas, any sweet music to compensate for the overblown emotionalism or the banality of the plot. Even I, totally immune to the pathology of love, do not escape being pestered by others whose attentions I have never solicited. The bane of my life at present is a woman who seems to have come straight from a mental hospital and landed on my doorstep. Several times a week I will find her following me down a street; she clutches at me, she tries repeatedly to kiss me, she writes long, obscene letters to me describing in explicit detail some programme of surrogate sex therapy which she offers with evangelical zeal with the aim of converting me from whatever I am to whatever she thinks I ought to be. Why, why? Because she *loves* me! She loves me so much that I have taken to talking to her as one would a pesky dog: 'Be off with you!' I will say (omitting the phrase 'my good woman' which I would normally use, not wishing to utter any words which she could misconstrue as endearing), trying to disengage her vice-like hand from my puny arm, while I race to catch the bus. My manners have deteriorated in direct proportion to the intensity and frequency of her demented overtures. On one occasion last summer following a performance of my Manhattan show, I had to be rescued from this woman (she had remained outside the theatre where I was performing and attacked me the moment I went out on the street), even the police were dragged in. It is extremely difficult to behave well if those around us are determined to provoke us into behaving badly, yet even so, we must constantly exercise our intelligence in devising strategies that will make our manners – literally – fool proof.

Saying 'no' ideally involves taking the blame upon oneself; that is, making yourself seem unworthy for some reason or by blaming outside circumstances. You may evoke God (if you dare), your parents, the neighbours, the objections of your husband (or wife) if you have one, the welfare of the children (if you have any), consideration for another lover, even, I suppose, the memory of a previous lover. In the last resort you could claim to be too frail, ill or mentally unstable to withstand the rigours of an affair. It should not be all that difficult to find some dramatic flaw in your character.

On the one hand you have to reassure your companion how wonderful, beautiful and desirable they are, but on the other, you have to explain why either the circumstances or some moral objection prevents you from accepting advances. A crude victory (getting home unscathed by battering your companion's ego) is no achievement. Like Miss Otis you must send your regrets. There is good in practically everyone so it is no hypocrisy to praise your companion's admirable qualities, or his one fine feature (if he is bereft of more than one), but you must also decline (for that is your wish) in such a way that any reasonable person would find your reservations believable and acceptable. Your companion may not, however, be reasonable (like the bag-lady who wants to bag me) and you might thus be obliged to draw the line, firmly but politely, against any further explanation of why you feel the way you do. If you have permitted intimacies in the past you can perhaps say that you now realize you don't have the constitution for such raptures and that you hope he will find someone better equipped to withstand the pitch of his passions, or if such comments will be taken with a pillar of salt, perhaps you could emphasize how *guilty* the liaison makes you feel and that you think it's really terrible to deceive poor old Stanley (it probably is) by having a flagrant affair behind his back. In short: you find a plausible but deeply personal reason why sexual intimacy cannot continue and place the 'blame' squarely on your own shoulders – at least until the door is closed and he is gone.

Some people only realize the true nature of a relationship when it ends; what has long been obvious to sceptical friends now becomes apparent to the pair who were formerly spellbound. When two people realize there is nothing further to be gained by pretending to be devoted to one another they frequently unleash a great gush of vindictive selfishness. Can nice manners modify emotional wreckage? Or are men and women doomed in their love affairs to be on their worst behaviour?

Given the brevity of most relationships, it makes sense that we never commit ourselves utterly to anything or anyone, no matter how much we may *say* we are utterly committed. We cannot impose stasis upon that which is dynamic – it is the folly of human history that so many men have thought otherwise. Instead of taking marriage vows that pledge undying devotion and then making a mockery of them, it would be better to enter a personal relationship with an acute sense of the provisional. Promising to do more than we are ever likely to fulfil only makes failure a certainty.

People would behave much more decently towards one another at the end of a relationship if they expected less to begin with. So one of the ways in which we can improve our manners in sexual relationships is by examining, and de-mythologizing, the process known as love.

Most books on manners, and all books on morals, prescribe 'Thou Shalts' and proscribe 'Thou Shalt Nots' as if edicts alone could alter behaviour. My contribution to this debate is based on trying to understand *why* people behave so badly and trying to devise strategies that either modify barbaric impulses at their source, or else, through defensive manners, afford some protection against the rudenesses of others.

If, instead of expecting love to endure for ever and ending up being outraged and devastated when it doesn't, we begin by expecting a relationship to be of limited duration (based on its agreeability and usefulness), we could then be pleasantly surprised by how long it lasts. If indeed it survives several years, a decade, or longer, it will do so because it keeps changing, corresponding to the changes in ourselves, and because it is self-corrective in areas that are problematic. In short: we must be willing to accept that even the dearest of friends and lovers are simply guests, free to leave at any time.

Given such an attitude towards others − you could call it 'love with a light touch' − we would never be tempted to speak ill of someone who has departed for greener mirages. When a former friend or lover is intent on becoming 'Ex-rated', instead of staging an hysterical scene, trying to bar his or her exit, one should whip out a scarf (preferably silk) and flap goodbye. The world is full of nuts and one is nearly bound to find someone else to leave slimy rings around the bathtub, burn holes in the carpet, scratch the records, dogear the books, leave crumbs all over the kitchen, and ruin one's peace of mind.

In tomorrow's world hellos and goodbyes will come at an even faster rate than they do today, so one may as well be prepared for a series of sunderings. Some people will react to this quickening of life's pulse by reaffirming traditional values such as the 'lifelong relationship' which only worked when the lifespan was short and temptations to wander were few. Others will declare the whole business of 'relationships' to be too difficult and instead embark on a series of callous affairs. As usual I occupy the middle ground: we should give to our dearest friends all that we can (which is almost certain to be more than they deserve), short of giving away our self-respect, in the cheerful knowledge that they are not likely to be with us for long. Every human transaction, however brief, should represent the best of which we are capable, so that we may say (when alone, for it is never to be boasted in the presence of others) that we did all that we could for whoever it was who needed us at that moment. It is a greater achievement to treat those closest to us with courtesy than it is to love them: few acts of violence are the result of etiquette but many are the crimes of passion.

When two people who once lived together, or were married or seemed about to be married, abandon their domestic treaties, part of the responsibility for maintaining good manners falls upon other people. Friends of such a severed couple must never mention one party to the other unless invited to do so and even then it is best to speak in terms that are fatuously bland. Friends should never create a situation in which two estranged people meet socially. You cannot invite a woman to meet her ex-husband (or instigate a meeting between any two people once intensely involved) unless you feel sufficient time has gone by for you to be able to mention that a party is being given at which circumstances have compelled you to invite her (or his) former partner and you feel obliged to ask, 'Will this embarrass you in any way?' Once, of course, 'sufficient time' meant ten years at least; now it might only be ten weeks.

Just as sexual relationships are entered into nowadays without much thought, so they are abandoned much more easily – at least in theory. However, it is not uncommon for people to enter into a relationship promising that there will be 'no strings' only to do their damndest to tie a noose around the other's neck. They espouse the 'new morality' going in but revert to the 'old morality' as soon as their interests are threatened. It is a frequent ploy of people who claim to be confused. Good manners require that we have a reliable knowledge of ourselves and refrain from victimizing others with our moods and emotions. That is Crisp's Second Law – if you're keeping track. You must always know what you want to do – and do it.

Upon saying this one evening to the audience attending my show, one woman got up and asked, 'But what can you do if you are genuinely confused? Or if someone else misleads you? How do you apply good manners to emotional insta-bility?'

'We can be sympathetic to a confused person,' I replied. 'But not indulgent.' A person who is prone to confusion in his life must recognize this and try never to involve others in it. He must adopt a more negative approach than most people, declining invitations he feels uneasy about, refusing to become involved in situations about which he has strong doubts, and refrain from associating with people about whom he is highly ambivalent. In short, it is the confused person who should pay the price (by leading a circumscribed social life), not those around him. When asked to make a commitment, a man who doesn't know five minutes ahead of time what he wants to do must say 'no', rather than 'yes' or respond with a convoluted 'maybe'. One can only hope that eventually he will become more certain about himself.

When such a man's confusion has created a particular doubt, he should try to behave in such a way that even if his confusion remains, he does not confuse anybody else. If he does not *know* whether he wants to meet next Friday to go to a movie, he must say 'no', even though later he may say to himself, Why the devil did I say that? I have nothing better to do on Friday. He must stick to what he said because he has no right to put anyone in the position where, at the last minute, he befuddles things by changing his mind.

I once knew a woman in London who hardly ever kept an appointment and even when she did, never arrived on time. Yet she would ring up every week or so, saying things like, 'Let's have lunch on Friday.' Rather than upbraid her for her perpetual tardiness and unreliability, I made it a practice to employ defensive manners so as not to become a victim of her confusion. I would simply say, 'It sounds marvellous. You come here, I'll be home from three to six, come what may, and we'll decide what to do when you get here.'

That made it sound as if I were making myself infinitely available, but in fact, I was drawing the line; I wasn't going to stand on a street corner and wait another half hour for her ever again. This way, whether she came or not was not a matter of consequence, I would be in anyway, enjoying the more dependable company of *The Times'* crossword puzzle. It is possible to circumvent other people's uncertainties by appearing to indulge them while actually curtailing their opportunities to make you dislike them.

We should never speak badly of people that we have *allowed* to behave badly. After three appointments that have not been kept, you only make the kind of appointments that you are free to ignore. This is more efficient and less taxing than going about complaining, 'That wretched woman never turns up. . . .' You must arrange matters so that a relationship is conducted on your terms. Good manners require that we understand enough of other people's behaviour (particularly that influenced by their weaknesses) to avoid being treated badly: we must know them better and faster than they do themselves and keep one step ahead, behind or sideways to preserve a margin of safety.

We are not free, however, to rebuke other people nor speak badly of them to others. To rebuke someone presupposes that we are above him in some way (at least that we are innocent of his type of folly though we may well be equally inconsiderate in some other way), but if it is true that we are superior to him, then the more challenging question is not 'Why does he behave so badly?' but 'Why do we associate with such a lower form of life?' As for complaining about someone behind his back – that is a particularly useless activity which changes nothing. Rather than advertise to the whole world that you are the victim of someone's misbehaviour you would be better employed asking yourself why you show such bad judgement in your relationships.

On several occasions during the latest run of my one-man show, members of the audience would ask me what I thought about the practice – often recommended by marriage counsellors – of trying to deal with problems in a relationship by having a frank discussion with the offended or offending party in an effort to produce an agreeable compromise. If a lifetime of observation of all-too-human squabbles means anything, I replied, my advice is: *never* have a frank discussion with anyone about anything. Let us apply this interdict to the problem we were wrestling with earlier, of how to say 'no' to someone who has sexual designs on your person when you have been known to say 'yes' on previous occasions, thereby creating an impression that commingling with his body, though it is unsightly, smelly and continually exudes a mixture of water and fat, is an agreeable prospect. Let us say that you have already gone out several times with a man, when he has wined and dined you, and you, for your part in the bargain, have popped into bed, but now realize that you don't want to have further sexual relations with the fellow.

You cannot say to the gentleman that you wouldn't mind having dinner with him but you don't want all that other stuff.

If you have allowed a ritual to be established which involves you-know-what, changing the terms will be difficult because, first of all, your decision affects the interests of someone else who clearly does not share your ethereal refinements, and secondly, because your shift in mood cannot be lucidly explained – it can only be rationalized, and at best you are likely to seem unconvincing. The trouble with having a brutally frank discussion with someone with whom you feel obliged to say, 'The rest of our relationship is fine but I'm afraid I'm tired of the sexual element,' is that he is likely to ring you up a few days later and tell you that you were 'in a bad mood'. And then you have to defend yourself and say that you were not in a bad mood, and that you truly, really, absolutely did mean that you don't want to go to bed with him again. So-called frank discussions rarely resolve problems. They frequently protract them – for in trying to put your feelings into words you will have introduced into the arena of public discussion all sorts of dredged-up bits of psychological seaweed that really ought to remain undisturbed at the bottom of your mental swamp. It will be no consolation to Randy Andy that the 'reason' you don't want to sleep with him any more is that he reminds you of your father, your brother or your pet dog. A frank discussion may not even work – and *then* where are you? All you will have done is introduce more divisive material for the two of you (to say nothing of bystanders) to analyse and argue about. Bang goes potential friendship.

The formula for achieving a successful relationship is simple: you should treat all disasters as if they were trivialities but never treat a triviality as if it were a disaster. If sex is a matter of great importance to your companion and of indifference to you, then don't argue about it: the sex-tax may be a nuisance to pay at times but it's long been part of the commerce between people and is often refunded through other benefits. If, however, your companion is absolutely tyrannized by his little dick-tator and you don't wish to share the yoke of sexual slavery, then you will have to separate –

but there is still no point in arguing about your differences.

It isn't so much the sex drive that makes people behave badly to one another, it is their egos: the view (or the unconscious attitude) that other people 'belong' to one, and that once they have taken a marriage vow or made any less formal but equally binding commitment, they are expected to remain subservient. The expression that 'all is fair in love and war' makes an equation that is no coincidence, for love *is* war conducted by other means. Instead of tanks mowing down our defences we are sabotaged by illusory promises. Instead of being wrestled to the ground by some roughneck conqueror we lie down of our own accord and are so brain-washed by the Ministry of Love that we even enjoy our surrender. Many's the unwed mother who can't figure out why a man has abandoned her after she gave him everything he wanted, when in fact it was only the struggle that intrigued her aggressor, not her individual self and certainly not the consequences of their concupiscent wargames.

There is nothing inherently angst-making about the act of sex; few men have been made miserable in a brothel. While I have little to say in favour of sex (it's vastly overrated, it's frequently unnecessary and it's messy), it is greatly to be preferred to the interminable torments of romantic agony through which two people tear one another limb from limb while professing altruistic devotion.

The message that 'love' will solve all of our problems is repeated incessantly in contemporary culture – like a philosophical tom tom. It would be closer to the truth to say that love is a contagious and virulent disease which leaves a victim in a state of near imbecility, paralysis, profound melancholia, and sometimes culminates in death. The next time some besotted swain tries drinking to you only with dilated pupils and whispers 'I love you,' into your ear, instead of being thrilled to the Wuthering Heights of your soul, look upon him with pity and regard him as stricken with the emotional equivalent of yellow fever. Or when the virus of love enflames *your* brain try to remember that grafting is for trees and cleaving is for snails and you are neither.

Our age is characterized by many strange beliefs and while the therapeutic value of love would probably top the list of our popular follies, the idea that 'communication' is beneficial to people would run a close second. According to this theory, the more people 'communicate' with one another, the better they will understand one another, and the more civilized their relationships will be. However, the quantity of communication, even the quality of communication, cannot improve any relationship if there is little of a positive nature to be said. When people of fixed ideas meet – be they Communist or Capitalist, Protestant or Catholic – the *less* they say about their peculiar obsessions the better. A courteous silence is more effective in keeping the peace than whole days of explanation, followed by whole weeks of explaining one's explanations. 'To know all is to understand all,' the saying goes. I would add, 'and be appalled by most of it.' This brings us to the issue of how much one person should tell another, when both are living together, of the seamier aspects of his life? Does a lover/friend/flatmate have a right to 'know' about what we think and do, or do good manners require that we shield our friends from knowing more than they can comfortably deal with?

When I was only English and lived in a rooming house in London, all the inmates became interested in a liaison between two of the residents. Some said that the young man was trifling with the affections of the girl, others that she was *allowing* the relationship to go too far. Then it was rumoured that the man had promised to marry the woman if he could get a divorce from a wife that no one had ever seen. When no divorce and no marriage took place, the young man's behaviour came in for a lot of criticism. Someone finally said, 'What else could he say – out of politeness?' It would seem we must consider the lie as a form of manners. It was too late for the young man to respect the young woman's virtue – tattered remnant though it was – but at least he could spare her feelings.

Good manners in affairs of the heart are a very tricky business. A man stays late at the office. When he returns home, a well-mannered wife does not ask where he has been or what he has been doing, but as well-mannered wives are as rare as the proverbial hen's tooth, the man must expect to be interrogated. He says that his activities would only bore his wife. In fact they absorb and infuriate her. She presses for further information. He says he has been filling in his income tax returns. He should have in his briefcase some evidence of this. Good manners demand that only substantiable lies are offered to our adversaries.

The wife should seem to be taken for a fool (if she is wise) and let the matter rest. He deceives her, she deceives him and all is well, for nobody is fooled for a moment. Now *that* is true understanding. For the man to tell his wife that he is having a sordid affair with his secretary is insulting, even if he adds that he did it because she was there and that she is in every way inferior to the wife. A nice reply would be: 'I respect you too much to sully our marriage with the truth,' but I cannot say what the consequences of this rejoinder would be.

Mr Nicholls went into this question many years ago in a revue called *A School for Husbands*. A married couple are sitting in a restaurant. The wife says, 'Do you think that woman over there is pretty?' The husband replies, 'What woman?' Full marks. When the wife indicates which woman she means he must not say 'no' if the person in question is a raving beauty – especially if the wife has indicated that she herself thinks the girl is most attractive. Good manners never admit of an outright contradiction. He says, 'Yes, but she doesn't appeal to me,' with a tender glance at his wife.

Most people would rather be treated courteously than be told the truth, and if you can add an imaginative flourish to your courtesy so much the better. Life is a game in which the rules are constantly changing; nothing spoils a game more than those who take it too seriously. Adultery? Phooey! You should never subjugate yourself to another nor seek the subjugation of someone else to yourself. If you follow that Crispian principle you will be able to say 'Phooey', too, instead of reaching for your gun when you fancy yourself betrayed.

Most of the advice given here implies that men and women are playing traditional sex roles – *he* is having an affair at the office, she is waiting for him at home. But the real world is always more complex than the pictures inside our heads. Now that women are 'liberated', and feel free to indicate that they are sexually available, the complications will be endless as women take less kindly to rejection than men.

When the 'new woman' says to a man, 'Let's go back to my place,' he may think to himself, well, I've enjoyed the evening but I don't really want to go home with this woman and stay up till three-in-the-morning in bed with her, so he has to find a way of excusing himself from the job of sex. This is more difficult for a man because he is *expected* to be utterly fascinated by sex.

He can't say, 'Oh, I have a terrible headache.' He can't say much of anything without seeming 'unmanly'. He has to make it clear that while she is eminently desirable he has his own special reason for declining the opportunity, yet his rejection must not convey any rejection of her, and this will be difficult because women have a special built-in antenna that picks up supersonic nuances. Perhaps if a man can say, with apparent kindness, 'I can't get involved at this time, in this way, my life is so complicated at the moment I really wouldn't like to take advantage. ...' he may get off the hook. He must not lay this on too thick, however, for she may be an advocate of the no-strings school of bedding and he's landed himself in trouble. And then, if he says, 'I don't want to get deeply involved at this moment,' there is nothing to prevent her from saying, 'You don't have to get involved! It'll only take ten minutes. Nothing to make an awful fuss about.' He will then be forced to feign such low tricks as passing out or coming down with a sudden attack of influenza. 'I may be old-fashioned ...' is a useful line of tack. Your companion may feel disconcerted about not having her whims gratified, but she can scarcely blame you, and certainly can't blame herself, if you appear to be behind the times.

The perfect date ends either agreeably in bed or agreeably not in bed; even on a non-sexual date a man must *look* at a woman as though he expected their relationship to be sexual but that this was not the right time or place, and she, for her part, returns the compliment and illusion of restraint. It is the *style* with which anything is said or done that matters most.

Some enchanted evening you may see a stranger across a crowded room – and if you remember what has been said here you may be able to ignore this latest opportunity for self-abasement. The spell will be broken. You will no longer expect your salvation to come from another as handsome as the sun. Instead you will have begun to live at peace with yourself, able to live with the knowledge that there is no salvation at all – only laughter in the dark.

8

The Wrong Stuff

'You lose your manners when you're poor.'
Lillian Hellmann, *Another Part of the Forest*

My home for the last two years has been in a rooming house on New York's East Third street, at the edge of what the natives call 'the DMZ Zone'. If I lived any further east I would have to travel to and from all social engagements in an armoured vehicle. My bedsitting room, at the top of the stairs on the third floor, is decorated in a style which befits my station in life: early Low Tech. I have a portable heater, a telephone and a hot-plate – all that I need to survive now that my life has become one long camping trip. I have no radio because my interest in Civil Defence is minimal and what else is radio good for? I have no television set because I don't see why I, of all people, should *pay* to take unreality seriously.

Visitors to my room often intimate that they find it cramped and suggest that I would be happier elsewhere, whereas I think that to have as much as 120 square feet in the heart – or rather, given my location, the kidney of Manhattan – is bliss, far beyond anything I dreamt for myself when I was young.

Sometimes these same visitors look out of my one window, which faces another wing of the house, and ask me if I wouldn't prefer a better view? Only unimaginative people need a view, but I don't say so. I like walls, I tell them, there are few things in life more reassuring than a wall, especially a blank one.

The wall I face is not perfect, however. There are two windows facing mine, so I do not escape reminders of other people. Sometimes, at night, any time after eleven, when I am huddling under my only lightbulb, a knock will come at my door or a verbal demand will pass right through it from my neighbour complaining that he cannot get to sleep with my light shining in his eyes.

To ask why he does not get a blind would be to raise the equally embarrassing question as to why I don't get one either. Rather than get embroiled in this rigmarole (for me the reason is that I don't see the point to investing in a blind, even one of Venetian quietude, when any day now I expect Life's curtain to fall) I have taken to putting out my light promptly by eleven p.m. If I come in later than that I undress in the dark, so as to spare my photosensitive neighbour any aggravation to his optic nerve. Living in proximity with other people requires that we consider their feelings, no matter how eccentric those feelings may seem to be, for that very eccentricity may be the essence of their identity. When my neighbour complains and I give way, or he notices that there is no longer any cause for offence, it may have little to do, in fact, with the alleged sleep-reducing glow of my wan sixty-watter, which after all has to penetrate two window-panes caked with soot before it impinges upon the retinas of his insomniacal eyes – it may be simply that he needs to exert his will and to savour the small victory of somebody obliging him. If something as little as the flick of a switch is enough to keep him docile then I am perfectly willing to liaise. It could be much worse: I could be living next door to a rock musician of the heavy metallurgical persuasion.

I am often asked by people why I am so patient with my enemies. The reason is partly habit and partly strategy. Having been the butt of mockery and abuse almost from birth I became well acquainted with humility and her twin, irony, even before my compulsory miseducation began in earnest. I would have died of exhaustion if I had tried to combat the treatment I received; instead I feigned not to be angry. This is the only method known to me by which one can survive one's emotions and also feign not to have them. It works. I am now almost entirely free from indignation. Apart from my run-ins with the amorous bag-lady, I can't remember the last time I 'answered back'. Other-cheekism is not only a way of purifying the soul, it is also part of every weak person's survival kit. If I had tried to defend myself in any of the street incidents of which in my youth I was the victim I might easily have been killed. I seem now to be in less physical danger than formerly but even when dealing with verbal harassment the principle is the same. Anyone, even with the thinnest layer of cerebral cortex, will recognize that we generally accomplish far more in social relations when we disarm an opponent through charm rather than bopping him on the nose or boxing his ears with verbal crudities.

Maintaining good manners is an emotionally taxing process. This is the principal reason why I live alone – the effort of constantly looking, saying and doing my best, or even my second best, would consume more energy than I am capable of replenishing in a twenty-four-hour period. My smile needs to have its battery recharged – otherwise I would start looking down-at-the-mouth like other people. I have often been offered the resistible opportunity of sharing a flat with someone – merging my cast-iron pots with her copper-bottomed pans in hot pursuit of the joy of cooking – but I steadfastly refuse all offers of 'round-the-clock companionship'. I need time alone and, besides, one should always be wary of anyone who promises that their love will last longer than a weekend.

I was asked one evening by a member of the audience what I thought of the idea of drawing up a contract at the outset of any relationship in which two people will live together. 'If I understand you correctly,' the man said, 'you recommend being clear with people ahead of time so that all parties will know where they stand, rather than squabbling over everything when your wife or husband, lover or room-mate has "lost that lovin' feeling"?'

'This is a very troubling area,' I replied. 'With some people, the only thing stronger than their lust is their greed, so that when they have tired of attacking our person they take aim at our purse.' A contract governing 'living arrangements' may be of some help in limiting the claims of those who are so ill mannered as to kiss-and-sue, but the growing reliance that all of us have on legal contracts of one sort or another, indeed our reliance on lawyers generally, is an admission that neither we nor the people we profess to love and cherish can be trusted to be fair and equitable in the event of a parting of the ways. As there is no consensus about good manners, and no consensus about moral values, we depend, more and more, on the law for authority, though the law in many cases is the opposite of what is moral, and seldom fulfils the requirements of good manners.

The law is simply expediency wearing a long white dress. In some counties, provinces or states, Dame Justice wears a different cut of dress and domestic delinquents are not above shopping around for whatever legal fashion best suits their designs. The law is resorted to mainly by unprincipled people as they have no other basis of behaviour. Good manners can never be coercive, or coerced. You cannot demand courtesy from people, you cannot penalize someone for failing to have a cheerful disposition. Good manners are given to the world, freely, by enlightened choice.

In a Kramer versus Kramer situation only *one* Kramer can win – though both may be right and certainly both have needs that a legal decision cannot satisfy. I generally regard anyone who conspires with a lawyer to create a lawsuit as someone who is making mischief for selfish reasons and who cannot get all that he or she wants through more civilized means. If one is not a scoundrel to start with, one will certainly be one by the time the case is over, for a lawsuit requires that both parties conceal as much as they can that may damage their 'side' while revealing as much as possible that will embarrass the other side. This contest between people, now made adversaries, has nothing to do with the truth, and nothing to do with maintaining peaceful relations.

So when I am asked for my opinion about 'marriage contracts' (or contracts governing any intimate relationship) I fail to see the purpose of signing a piece of paper that it would be ungracious and unseemly for me ever to enforce. I do say, though, to those who want to hedge their vows of undying love with practical considerations, that one should never draw up a legal contract on one's own account with anybody. Rather, you must produce someone else who 'insists' on it, blaming your father, or your brother, or your manager or your agent, someone who insists on safeguarding your interests while you yourself must be presented as being much too loving, much too spiritual, much too beautiful in nature to expect anything legal to be brought into the situation.

There must not be any undignified squabble even in private and certainly not in public, about finances or possessions, when you withdraw from a relationship, or when someone else withdraws. The only time that you are free to act like a born-again capitalist, announcing to the world that you prefer money to people, is *before* a relationship has begun. If you choose badly in your bedmates and companions, there is no responsible option but to pay the price, whatever that may be.

I recommend having no relationships except those easily borne and disposed of; I recommend limiting one's involvement in other people's lives to a pleasantly scant minimum. This may seem too stoical a position in these madly passionate times, but madly passionate people rarely make good on their madly passionate promises. Few people seem to be able to conduct their personal relationships with much style or grace. Once you are past the first few bars of their overtures, it's the same old song-and-dance, the same step forward, two steps back, a steady regression into banality and pettiness. The reason that so many human transactions end in corruscating bitterness is that genuine goodwill among people is in short supply. But we can compensate for this deficiency through good manners, and create the *appearance* of goodwill. Those people who insist – as if it were a startling revelation – that manners are a form of hypocrisy and that we should feel free to express what we truly feel no matter what the occasion, are naïve about human nature. There isn't enough *natural* good feeling to go around to keep social relations running smoothly and we require the artificial sweeteners of manners. I am not of sweeter disposition than most people (if anything, the frail and the elderly have *more* cause for sourness than the young but have less means of expressing their frustration) but I may *seem* to be kinder and more patient because I have learned to conserve my strength for the most trying situations rather than fritter away my emotional energy on trifles and run around like a nervous wreck with a low tolerance for stress. Good manners are a result of knowing one's strengths and weaknesses, and through that self-knowledge one can devise clear, conscious policies about what constitutes the main chance in a wide variety of circumstances. It is more important to develop a general attitude of gracious respect for others than it is to swear by some weighty tome of codified behaviour which is then used as Holy Writ to condemn others for their infractions. Given an attitude of pragmatic respect for others you may not do the perfect thing according to Debrett or Miss Manners, but you will likely do a much better thing than people normally do when they follow their emotional vagaries. To be considerate towards others requires no rules but it does require a sharpened presence of mind. If this modest book contributes to such an exalted condition in readers I will have the blissful satisfaction of knowing that what *Jane Fonda's Workout Book* does for flabby stomachs my spiritual exercises have done for sloppy minds.

I propose that we consider three examples of common mistakes in social relations, each involving one of the pitfalls of human misbehaviour: the lust for power, the lust for money and just plain lust. The common denominator in each case is that one party wants something from another and will stop at nothing to get it; whenever we confront an unbridled desire we are surely in the presence of a tragedy-in-the-making.

The first example is a variant of the issue we have already discussed – trying to find well-mannered ways to protect one's virtue when it is under siege. A friend of mine, an actress of even greater beauty than talent, complained to me that she is frequently exposed to compromising situations; sex on the job, to be blunt, or employment in exchange for ravishment. Sexual discrimination is a more complex problem than simply receiving a warm offer from an overheated suitor, indeed feelings of affection are likely to be absent in sexually oriented power-plays. Though sex may be the means of an employer's domination, something else is what he is really after: the submission and humiliation of a subordinate. This makes his motives even more impure and his designs even less acceptable than those of an average Lothario. Anyone with power (money and/or influence) who uses that power to pin down the powerless is a cad, of course, but something other than name-calling is required to keep his aggressiveness in check.

My actress-friend tells me that in the arts employment often hangs by a slender thread on the end of which dangles a proposition. The extremes for anyone in her profession are: either you want the part so badly you are willing to sleep with just about anyone at least once (though my advice is don't start with the janitorial staff), or you don't want the part at all and aren't willing to 'trade-off' with anyone. Then there is the twilight zone: you would love to have the part and the person with whom you are trying to ingratiate yourself isn't too objectionable although you would rather be given the role without the obligatory roll.

If we are speaking of the man (whose minimal sense of decency we can only appeal to), it is up to him to let you know before you get the part that he intends to exact his pound of flesh – that while you may be a fearsomely magnificent Lady Macbeth on stage you are expected to be as sexually subservient as the anti-heroine of *The Story of O* backstage. Even a cad should be willing to give a sporting chance to his prey. He should then say, 'I'll recommend you strongly for this role, I think we're going to be great friends,' or whatever. That gives you a crawlspace in which to manoeuvre. You are free to say, 'I long for the role but I would like to be considered a serious actress. I do hope that our personal relationship, whatever it may become, will not influence you or anyone else to whom you may recommend me.' In an imperfect world that will do, everything is clear and *you* have the choice.

But your Phantom of the Theatre may not say much of anything. He may recommend you strongly and you may get the part, but then there comes an undignified aftermath in which he says, 'Well, how do you think you got it? Why do you think I recommended you? You're a mediocre actress, at best, and if it weren't for me, you wouldn't be on the stage. The least you can do in return is ...'

Caught, she then has to try to find a way of saying that she is grateful for any influence he may have used, and purpose he has served, but that from that point on she will make her own way and will try to justify his faith in her – thus forestalling any further deterioration of what is already an undignified scene. She has to imply that her return for any influence he may have shown is her undying gratitude. Then, virtue intact, she hot-foots it out.

She must never suggest that she *might* pop into bed with him when she has no intention of doing so. Even when she arrives in his office and allows him to give her the most perfunctory kiss, she is then guilty of leading him on. As a part-time thespian I am well aware that in the theatre 'kissing' is a problem because everybody kisses everybody, so you have to make sure if you are giving or receiving kisses in a promiscuous profession that they are just osculatory tokens.

The leading lady who does not want to end up in Sam Shepherd's flock, or Joseph Papp's lap must find a way of saying, 'I hope that this is not part of the bargain.' Obviously she can't blurt out, 'I'm an actress, not a whore ...' because some producers don't know the difference. She must find a way of being accepted for her talent alone, or her talent first if not alone, and the best way of achieving this is by being clear with her prospective employers with whom she must be agreeable but never coy. In Victorian times in England, as described in a scene from George Meredith's *The Egoist*, a well-bred young woman was expected to be so alert to the more predictable patterns of male behaviour that it was considered a lapse on her part if she even received a proposal of marriage that she had no intention of accepting. She was expected to head off any unwelcome suggestions because good manners require that nobody be made a fool of and, if possible, nobody must ever be put in a position where he is refused. This is best accomplished by preventing anyone from asking an embarrassing question. When a man said to a Victorian heroine such as we find in *The Egoist*, 'Thank goodness we're alone, there's a serious matter I wish to discuss with you,' sensing that this may be a marriage proposal she would head him off by replying, 'Oh please Reggie, don't discuss anything serious with me, you know what a frivolous person I am.' If he persists ('Dammit, you can be serious just this once') she too persists ('What? – and spoil a perfect record of levity?'). With any luck the more astute of the two in this exchange will prevail. Her meaning will be perceived and politely accepted.

My actress-friend says that if producers or directors said to her, 'Come sit on my knee while you read these lines,' at least she would know what she was in for; but just as a Personnel Manager is unlikely these days to say to a pretty applicant for an office job, 'Cover up your knees young lady, you will only get *this* job based on your typing speed,' the role of sex, and the use of sex, in any power-play between employer and employee is frequently covert in the beginning, and therefore misleading. No matter how indifferent or platonically benign a male employer may seem to be, one should always keep an eye out for his snake in the grass. A passing reference, once again, must be made on behalf of those who plead diminished responsibility for everything they do on the grounds that they are chronically confused. It could happen that a young woman actually *does* wish to be seduced by her boss or fancies that something of his executive lustre will rub off on her between the sheets, but that as the seduction proceeds she realizes she has undertaken more than she bargained for. To someone who is totally innocent, sex may seem like two angels holding hands, it may seem much milder, nicer, sweeter than it actually is, whereas once she gets into the throes of lunge-and-plunge she may discover how revolting sex can be and often is (and how painful, I might add) so that she is literally on the horn of a dilemma. My advice to the first-time person is never embark on any seductions, no matter what the bad poetry of perfume advertisements may have led you to believe. With luck you may never know just how awful sex can be. That is my last word – well, almost – on the subject of sex (which I dwell upon only because there is a need to deflate the overrated, and nothing in our culture, not even home computers, is more overrated than the epidermal felicity of two featherless bipeds in desperate congress).

My final advice to my actress-friend (and anyone else who faces the perils of sex-on-the-job) was that she should make it known tactfully and early to her prospective employer that she is happily involved with a lover or husband (whom she need never produce) and that she could not begin to contemplate 'sleeping around' to advance her career. The world loves a lover, as the saying goes, and even the most unprincipled artistic director or producer is likely to respect, albeit grudgingly, not so much the rights of a woman in love but the 'rights' of another man. Such a subterfuge may not be a fail-safe method of preventing harassment by a sexually aggress-ive boss but it should reduce both the number and the intensity of his lewd manipulations. It may well be that more skill is required to manage one's backstage ploys than is required for the onstage plays – but such is life in the theatre, sordid and venal like everything else.

We come now to the second most divisive issue among people: money. As with sex, the reason that money causes so many fallings-out between people is that a large component of selfishness is involved; and, as with sex, my advice is starkly simple: it is a great mistake to borrow money from people and an even greater mistake to lend it. But such things happen, especially in today's economy – which is brought about by citizens following the example of their governments and *leaping* into a bottomless pit of debt. Were it not for the costly ventures of wars, ranging from Vietnam to the Falk-land Islands, many Western countries would be in much better financial shape than they are, but when dealing with politicians, as I have observed for seventy-five years, the obvious is something which they discover only after they have exhausted every other explanation.

Indebtedness is unwise but it is also fashionable so we are bound to see a great deal more of it, and where the personal finances of spouses/lovers/friends/flatmates are concerned we are likely to see a great deal of ill-tempered squabbling over money and who owes what to whom. These are some of the ways which may help to keep such relationships smooth. First of all, one should try to get out of allowing anyone to borrow anything at all by forestalling demands. Usually when someone is about to put 'the touch' on you, there will be some sort of preamble broadly hinting at his impecunious state. He won't just rush up to you and say, 'Lend me £500.' He will have to explain that he is in a great predicament and doesn't know how to deal with it, that he has absurdly allowed himself to run short of cash – and so on. As soon as you perceive the direction in which he is headed you must make a counter-move and put up a roadblock of defensive manners. You sympathize, you know all too well about the spiralling cost of living, you too are running desperately short but believe that it is better to 'tighten one's belt' than to rack up huge debts on credit. You must make it clear, as a general policy, that you do not believe in borrowing money, and certainly aren't in any position to lend it. You are free to invent an excuse for not lending money (and/or property) but the excuse must cast no aspersion upon the person with his hand out. Then change the subject cheerfully to show (if you wish to) that in all other respects you are a good friend interested in his welfare.

If you *do* lend money you have to lend it gladly or not at all. You cannot ask what the money is for (it is now *his* money and *his* business); you must never state when you want it back (the other person must say when he will pay you back), in fact you have to recognize that you've given up the whole thing voluntarily. You should never lend what you are not prepared to lose. The hard times of your friend, whatever the cause, may continue long beyond his original expectations. He may even not be able to repay you at all. If you insist that he gave his word, and that you absolutely relied upon getting the money back at a certain time, you will only end up frustrating yourself and adding to the distress of your friend. There are only two ways of avoiding such a contretemps: either you do not lend anything under any circumstances, or else you lend, in such amounts and to such people, only that which you are willing to bestow as a gift. Either money is too important to you to lend or else it is too unimportant to worry about.

As I have never borrowed from anyone I have no experiences as a debtor, but in my solicitations for material from others for this book, in the areas of modern social life where manners are needed most, the subject of money was clearly a sore one. 'There's nothing like money to bring out the wrong stuff in people,' said one young man in the audience of my show. By 'the wrong stuff', he explained, he meant all that is petty and meanspirited in human beings, all that is paranoid and vindictive. He related the saga of a personal loan which he had obtained from a former friend, now paid in full but not before the friendship was ruined. I regarded his story as a grotesque soap opera and found it hard to believe that fully grown people could be so childish, but when he was finished others in the audience affirmed that what they had heard was a common tale among common men where common currency is involved.

His friend, the man explained, was a middle-aged bachelor – a former priest, a former social worker, a former manager of a bookstore specializing in texts on Bhuddism and Eastern enlightenment.

Apparently these erstwhile occupations inspired confidence in the young man. It was the frequency of the word 'former' that *I* found ominous. This friend, the man said, not only agreed to lend him $1000 in a tight spot, but offered it even before the money had ever been asked for, and had said things like, 'If there's ever anything I can do, let me know,' and 'Well, that's what friends are for, aren't they?' He had created an emotional climate that made borrowing seem more than acceptable, almost part of their friendship. When the money was finally requested, it was promptly sent. There would be no interest charged of course. There was no stipulation as to when the money would be repaid, simply one understanding friend saying to another, 'Repay me when you can.'

But in about two months' time the first long-distance phone call came in which the friend asked if he would be getting his money back soon. The young man said that he was startled. He'd thought that 'as soon as possible' meant somewhere between 'no rush' and a year. His friend went on to cite a number of pending expenses which he must soon pay (taxes, fire insurance etc.). The young man promised to do what he could – knowing well there was little he *could* do. He said that it occurred to him that this unexpected request for payment was perhaps a ploy through which his friend was testing the strength or the quality of their emotional bond but, in any case, he had no more funds at that moment than when he had borrowed the money, and now felt resentment towards the friend for having given him a false sense of security.

The phone calls became more frequent, and with each one the emotional strain increased; letters soon began to follow and the rhetoric grew more reckless with each passing exchange. The young man repeatedly explained that he had no money, and no prospects of getting money for several months at least, but promised to repay at the first opportunity. This was not good enough. Allusions to taking legal action were made. The friend also reminded the young man that if he had gone to a bank he would have had to pay stiff interest. The implication of this last being that the young man should offer to pay a bonus to his former friend, who was now devolving into a mere acquaintance, or at least promise in writing to do so. The communications which he now received (dreading every one) were reproachful and strident. He would get letters saying things like: 'You must send me some money soon. This is becoming insufferable. My summer plans are f**ked up because of this and it is all your fault. I am charging you 10 per cent interest from this point on. This is more than fair ...'

Finally the young man came up with a date on which he could repay, sent his former acquaintance a post-dated cheque and a curt note saying don't pester me further, but even this was not enough. The one-time friend wrote back demanding that he be paid $25.43 (or thereabouts – I pull the figure from the air) for banking and long-distance telephone charges said to be related to the debt. So the young man dispatched a money order in exasperation. That was not enough. A few days later he received a long letter on official stationery from a lawyer saying that he had advised his client – the former Mr Enlightenment 'to attend at your bank, pursuant to my instructions, on the date of your post-dated cheque to have it certified, and if the funds are not available at that time, proceedings will be commenced against you immediately and without further notice for the collection of the amount in question'. None of this legal bullying was necessary, the young man paid as he said he would, and at last the belligerence ceased.

All that this gratuitously overwrought drama suggests is that money is more important than people and the most treacherous friend that a man can have is one who does *not* know this truth about himself and who poses as someone who is spiritually advanced and generous in nature, when, in fact, he is just as ruthlessly materialistic and money-grubbing as a bill collector. The young gentleman in question should never have borrowed the money, he should have lived within his means; but having made the mistake of becoming indebted to another, he seems to have behaved as well as one could hope. He did repay the sum at the first opportunity, which was precisely what he had promised originally, and he refused to escalate the war by insulting the man who was hounding him. The trouble with linking money with friendship is that as long as the friendship flourishes the debt may be forgiven, but if something happens to the friendship (even if it simply expires from boredom) any outstanding debts are likely to be pursued vindictively, with a vengeance and a persistence that no bank would ever resort to, for all the once positively charged emotions that fuelled the friendship now run the opposite way.

As I noted earlier, only unprincipled people turn to the law for authority; people with 'the right stuff' solve their own problems amiably, like adults, and always with good manners. In future it would be in everyone's best interests if this gentleman (and others like him) adds 'former money-lender' to all the other earlier roles in life for which he was so unsuited.

Even when the money was repaid the young man continued to meet with social embarrassments as a result of this loan, for it turned out that his big-hearted friend was even larger of mouth and had broadcast and dramatized for months the details of his dilemma: his roof was leaking and he couldn't afford to fix it, his car needed repairs but he couldn't pay the garage, he was in arrears at his bank, he had had to borrow a large sum to make ends meet – all because of the young man's tardiness in repaying what he owed. Mutual friends and even innocent bystanders were hectored with unending tales of woe, as he went about complaining in high dudgeon that he had been betrayed and abused, just like King Lear. No one was rash enough to ask him how a loan of only $1000 could possibly cause such havoc. Surely the lack of *this* could not account for *all* of his financial troubles, and when the debt was paid he made no comparable effort to inform the same people that all was now well. Finally the young man complained to his former friend about his indiscretion in telling so many people of what he had presumed was a private matter between them. He received the snapping rejoinder, 'I've never said anything I wouldn't say to your face!'

The idea that one is willing to say something terrible to somebody's face is no justification for saying it, either to their face or behind their back. If anything, the breach of manners is greater if you say nasty things to the face, for you are then deliberately creating an embarrassing and potentially public situation. So if you are determined to speak evil of people you *must* do so behind their backs. You just have to hope that what you say isn't reported. In any case the breach of manners then passes to the person who repeats what you have said.

No well-bred person ever sues anybody for anything – be it money or redress for some imaginary damage done to 'reputation'. Suing people only makes one unpopular: resorting to the law to resolve a dispute is a declaration of spiritual bankruptcy. One is saying in effect, 'I do not have the time, patience, good manners and diplomatic skills to resolve this problem therefore I will take refuge in the law.'

I used examples of this kind (to illustrate the lower depths of mankind where money is concerned) during my American tour in the autumn and winter of 1983–84: playing in Chicago, New Orleans, and other but no less sociologically fascinating places like Austin, Texas. I was a Manners-Mobile going about the United States doing my bit to raise the tone during a period of history in which many people seem to be lost at sea without rules, radar or rudders. I didn't give (nor do I offer readers now) strict navigational instructions. I merely provided a lighthouse beacon by which others might set their own courses.

One night in Chicago a young woman said, 'Some of the things you say make sense to me in the context in which you give them, but then when I think about some other application of your advice, I find myself unsure about its soundness. For instance, if we are never to speak badly of anyone publicly, what does that say about politicians, or journalists? Could anyone belong to those professions if they were well mannered?'

There are certain occupational groups which are traditionally exempt from manners: gangsters, for instance, though nowadays even a gangster will spend more time advancing his aims (which are often indistinguishable from those of big 'legal' business) through skilfully conducted social activities than through anti-social acts of violence. We are nearing the point in this era of artificial intelligence and electronic sophistication where crude strength and a macho attitude are a liability. I believe that in the future it will be those who are patient and polite in a language that a computer understands who will advance, whereas those who are rude and aggressive will make a lot of noise, perhaps do considerable damage, and get nowhere.

Gangsters, politicians, and business executives would all benefit from having better manners, but frequently in their lust for power, men of such occupations do not act in their own best interests. They forget to cloak their daggers.

There is a certain kind of man who if he once sees a John Wayne movie in his youth will for ever after be rushing into harm's way with his adult spurs spinning and guns blasting. Vietnam, Falkland Islands, Grenada, Beirut, you name it. Modern life in many parts of the world simply imitates B-movies from Hollywood in the 1940s, except that as Gloria Swanson noted in *Sunset Boulevard*, the movies didn't get bigger, it was the stars who got smaller. So now we have amateur theatres of war all over the globe, and rep theatre terrorists in every shopping centre practically tripping over their bombs, issuing garbled communiqués to the mass media saying things like, 'We the Have-Nots take full irresponsibility for killing two pensioners and their grandchildren by blowing up Santa's Toyland at Dickens and Jones this morning in the name of freedom'. I've never met a self-admitted terrorist, they seem to be closety types, but I would be surprised to meet one with a grasp of anything other than explosives. How anyone's aims could be advanced by blowing up people unrelated to one's oppression is a mystery to me. As someone who has been oppressed and exploited for most of my life, I'm more than entitled to an arsenal of letter-bombs and other destructive devices, but I have never had the slightest interest, apart from the occasional violent fantasy, in killing, torturing and maiming those who have hurt me.

This may be partly because *I* never liked John Wayne movies but is mainly because I don't want to imitate my enemies in their behaviour. Some battles are better lost with one's self-respect intact than won by means which leave one's identity in tatters.

Now let us push onwards and downwards to the press club. All journalism is ill mannered, all journalists must expect to be considered as lacking in taste and breeding. In England, most people try not to let journalists into their homes at all because they know perfectly well that they will be written about and, in England, unless you are a Sex Pistol running about half-cocked, no publicity is wholly good. In America, I don't think it matters so much. People do seem to be willing to be written about and even encourage it as proof of their existence. In either case, whether you've brought it upon yourself or are quite innocent in the matter, journalism is a rude activity – the intellectual equivalent of breaking wind in public.

My final example of 'the wrong stuff' involves a family so sensitive to its standing in a certain community that it threatened to launch a lawsuit against a publisher for having run an article which they found embarrassing. The article did not mention the family by name, indeed no one who was not already unusually familiar with the facts that were disclosed could have begun to guess the identity of the family, but that did not prevent the mother-and-son team from charging forth and hiring a lawyer to preserve the remnants of family honour. As a motive for misbehaviour, 'social status' runs a poor third to 'money' and 'sex' but it is still the origin of many a brouhaha. When someone feels that their 'reputation' has been harmed in some way, revenge against the offending party can become as intensely passionate as three or four of the deadly sins combined. I maintain that whatever you hear about yourself you should not challenge it. If you are truly a good person and your goodness is apparent to most people who meet you, why on earth should you pay the slightest attention to a rumour, or even a public allegation? It is only people who crave a reputation which they do not deserve who must call in lawyers to preserve appearances. A lawsuit is the twentieth-century equivalent of a duel and like a duel it proves nothing (only in movies is the best man the best shot) while engorging the emotions of all concerned, making everyone think the blackest thoughts about the 'opposite side'. A lawsuit is a deliberate act of rudeness carried out by proxies, and the reason why people hire proxies to do their dirty work is that they *know* that what they are doing is wrong and *rude* but they feel less responsibility if they are not directly involved in the confrontation. It is usually well-educated people who resort to lawsuits (people of the lower classes when offended still rely on the old bop on the nose), which in my view compounds their error, for in setting the machinations of legal mischief in motion they are confessing that their education, their professed interest in culture and the humanities, is a fraud. I believe that two people of goodwill can solve *any* problem. When this does not happen, when one party gets on his or her high-horse of indignation and declares the other party a scoundrel, then we are in the presence of human perversity, and human tragedy.

There is no doubt that the journalist at the wormy core of this story is a writer of the worst sort – an undistinguished graduate of the George Orwell school. Such writers often fancy themselves as thought-provoking, socially conscious agitators but usually they will settle for any response from a reader whom they pin down with lurid disclosures, box his ears with facts he doesn't want to know, pummel him with paranoia, torture him with conspiracy theories, and then, when the reader is so overwhelmed and alarmed that he can barely speak, the writer will expect some journalism award.

The journalist in my example had for some years cultivated a reputation for delving into the seamier aspects of the human condition. The family that he became acquainted with was well aware of his sensationalistic bent – with the exception of Father Bear, an academic poetaster of greater pretension than talent, who made a point of not knowing anything that appeared in the 'popular press' unless he was told that it was a favourable review of one of his books. Mother Bear, the flag-bearing liberal of the family (she *had* to be a liberal in view of the way her children turned out), was not only familiar with this journalist's work but appreciative of it. What possible merit there could be, however, in stories with titles like 'Peter Pan at 27' (a profile of a famous figure skater) or 'Who's Afraid of Sharon Pollock?' (practically everybody according to the author), or 'Will Success Spoil . . .?' (fill in the name of the latest person to be overrated by the press and then demeaned – journalists get you coming *and* going), is to me a matter of conjecture.

Arthur Bell of *The Village Voice* calls this kind of writing 'dishing the dirt'. Few, actually, 'dish' quite like Mr Bell, but the charms of gossip are lost on me because I naturally assume that most people are terribly depraved and corrupt and it comes as no surprise to hear the details. What really does astonish me is to hear about someone, other than Mother Theresa, doing something really nice for someone with no strings attached.

At any rate the journalist was introduced to this august family through its weakest kink – a young man who placed an advertisement for his 'services' in the personal ads of the local newspaper. The journalist, always on the lookout for salacious new material, answered the ad and received a card in reply. The young man boasted of the dimensions of his 'equipment' and gave the family number.

A relationship of sorts between the journalist and the young man existed for about two months, during which the journalist pumped the young man for every possible scrap of information he might have on the underground of male prostitution. He told the young man that he was working on a piece which would investigate several crimes that had come to his attention, instances in which male prostitutes had 'ripped off' their clients. He saw this as some form of class struggle, and he was going to quote Mr Marx and Ms Emma Goldman, and who knows who else, to give the article intellectual tone, even though it would be basically just another sewerpiece.

Fate intervened. A 73-year-old man, who ought to have known better was murdered and robbed by a 17-year-old 'street kid'. The journalist, with his parson's nose for news, decided that here was a case that deserved the *In Cold Blood* treatment. He sold his editor on his idea of doing a four-part series on the crime, one of which would investigate the shadowy world of male prostitutes; who they are, where they come from, and what sort of code they live by.

By now this paint-by-number picture should be taking nascent form. As one of several sources on the subject of male prostitution, the journalist quoted comments made by the downstanding son of this upstanding family and alluded to him as a 'red-haired, 23-year-old' called 'Nick'. (Other male prostitutes with false names were also quoted.)

A few days after the particularly contentious article was published, the editor received an urgent call from a lawyer, conveying the message that Mother Bear and Baby Bear were going to sue his publication for every penny they could (odd how the morally wounded turn to money for consolation, don't you think?) on the grounds that the article was malicious and defamatory. These are catch-all phrases (how can anyone of no distinction be defamed?), but when a lawyer uses them, one is obliged to pay attention not because of any *real* merit in his argument outside the world of law but because once the courts are dragged in to settle a dispute the weird intricacies of law supersede all other considerations.

The family's case rested mainly on two contentions; that the journalist had not made it official that he was gathering information for a story to be published when he talked informally with family members; and they alleged that the existence of a number of personal letters from the journalist to the young man proved that there was a compromising relationship between them, ending in a quarrel before the story was written. Finally that the journalist had therefore written his 'exposé' out of malice.

The editor was shown several of these letters by the lawyer, and giving them a quick glance, he found them embarrassingly poetic ('What a great pleasure it is to find someone who understands ... etc.') and being a 'man's man' who would never say anything poetic to anyone, he concluded that the letters were indeed suspect, and that it would be difficult to *prove* in court that the published article did not contain any revenge or malice.

The journalist argued that no one disputed the *facts* of the article, and thereby threw the young man's 'rate card' for services (handwritten and signed) into the public ring. If the facts are not in dispute, then the means by which he obtained his information were irrelevant, he contended. Investigative journalists have to employ some undercover techniques to get the information they seek.

By now the publisher too was fuming, for he had received an unencouraging report from the editor saying that, in his opinion, the journalist had behaved unprofessionally at best, and something much worse at worst. He had heard from *his* lawyer, who said that such a case was bound to be messy, probably prolonged and would cost at least $10,000 just to enter the ring for round one at the lowest local court. It would cost ten times that amount if one fought one's way to the Supreme Court championships. Not feeling inclined to play Rocky, least of all over something sodden with heavy whiffs of perversion, the publisher said: 'What do they want? Let's settle this matter quickly.'

What the family wanted – though I find this hard to believe of anyone with an IQ of over 80 – was for the newspaper to print an apology and a retraction saying that the young man named as 'Nick' in the series was not to be mistaken for 'Baby Bear' of such-and-such an address. In other words, the family wanted, simultaneously, a public declaration of its identity and a public disavowal that they were the family in question. No one else, not even the editor or publisher, both of whom were well informed about their social community, could ever have guessed from the passing reference in the article who the young man was or where he lived. Only people who already knew the details of the young man's life, or who knew of his relationship with the journalist, would have been able to even speculate about his identity, and no one can be defamed among people who already know his secrets.

As with most disgraceful behaviour, once a person embarks on a destructive course there can never be a cleansing result. The newspaper did publish a retraction (which was untrue). The family, presumably, preserved its illusions of dignity (based on getting a newspaper to publish a false statement). Now far more people knew about the case and subsequently spread the rumours far and wide, so that, in a sense, the greatest damage that was done to this family was done by its own defensive weapons. The journalist went on, convinced more than ever that his bosses were craven hypocrites, and now gives guest lectures at journalism schools where he uses such examples to prepare the students for 'the real world' where 'it never rains but pisses corruption'.

So, the trouble with lawsuits, as with most forms of rudeness, is that they do not work. Suing a person to claim money is not likely to end in your receiving repayment any faster than you would normally. Indeed remaining friends with someone over a difficult period is much more likely to preserve goodwill and earn gratitude, whereas an atmosphere of paranoid confrontation is likely to make for 'bad vibes'. Suing a person to protect your good name is even more self-defeating; such an action reveals that you are insecure and feel that you require some external authority to declare you to be a lady even if you are a tramp. Furthermore, you will probably be required to reveal a great deal more unsavoury faces and info (you weren't drunk on 5 January as the story alleged but you *were* stoned every other night that week) than the original slander contained, so that you may well win the battle but lose the war. A lawsuit brings out the worst in *everybody*, and anyone who chooses to *increase* the incivility of modern life is a reprehensible rogue indeed, no matter what ideals motivate his actions. There is little justification for most of the misunderstandings between people and there is never any justification for conducting a private quarrel in public.

Sexual manipulation, financial manipulation, and legal manipulation – these are the most common ways in which people of 'the wrong stuff' try to gain power. If I were the actress in that long ago first example I would say to the amorous producer, 'I am deeply flattered by your attentions, but I am even more deeply involved in an important relationship and I couldn't possibly be unfaithful to him. Besides it's deeply important [to an actress everything is deep] for me to gain recognition on the basis of whatever talent I have.' Even if your boss has a reptilian aspect that gives you the willies, you are obliged to flatter him slightly while making your negative message clear. Villains, too, have feelings.

In the second case, I would make a clear-cut decision, when asked for a loan, as to whether it is money that is sacred or whether it is people who are paramount. If I chose the first, I would decline the loan. If I chose the second course, the money would be of no consequence to me, and it would be a pleasant surprise to be repaid when my friend could afford it.

If I were the supposedly injured party of the third case I would first ask myself calmly: are these statements true, and if so, what is to be gained by trying to discredit the journalist who wrote them? Actually this problem would never arise with me as I have divulged too much about myself already to be of any interest to investigative journalists. Trying to turn attention away from themselves by attacking the journalist's motives for writing the story may have worked in the example given (at least for a time it shook the confidence of the editor and the publisher in the journalist's 'objectivity') but the cost was greater than anything gained. In threatening to launch a lawsuit, even if it was only a threat and not sincerely intended, the family became the object of many a salacious tidbit on the grapevine. (It is possible that this family simply wanted to advance to legal step one, and expose the journalist's correspondence to his employers, without intending ever to go to legal step two where they would have been required to hang out their dirty laundry in a court of law.)

I can well imagine a middle-aged woman reading this book (the immature aren't likely to be interested, and the criminally insane are exempt from reading it) and saying to her husband, 'See, dear, Mr Crisp says that one should never sue anybody. *He* says all conversations should aspire to be pleasant – even when the business at hand is unpleasant and the people you are dealing with are hopelessly neurotic.' And the husband may say, 'I don't care what some old poof has to say about anything.' The woman, who has read the text closely will reply, 'Mr Crisp says that you can't judge the worth of an idea by its origin. *He* says that many people persist in being pushy and rude because they think that their tactics are effective, whereas they have never compared how much further they might get if they were more considerate and polite.'

Indeed, to one and all of the 'wrong stuff' these are my parting words: *Every time we speak we can make some situation better or we can make it worse.* Either one works, little by little, day by day, to raise the tone of social life within one's sphere of influence, or one ends up, carelessly or deliberately, exacerbating the relationships of which one is part, making most or all of them function less well, less smoothly, and lowering the level of social life. It is this simple: you bring light to the lives of others or else you bring darkness. Either you have a concept of what constitutes good behaviour in your relations with others and feel ashamed when your manners fail, or when you fail your manners, or else the truth about you is that you are not a good person and never will be, and anyone of common sense should abandon you and run hatless into the street when they see you coming.

There are even people so perverse that *after* they have treated you badly and exposed you to all sorts of embarrassment and harassment they will ring and suggest that you meet them for drinks and a few words of conciliation. *Don't go.* Stay put whatever you do. Once a person has treated you badly (I mean really badly, not merely being late for the theatre or getting drunk and pressing your knee), chances are that your forgiveness will only make him incorrigible. He will sin and beg forgiveness, then sin again and beg for more forgiveness, and then sin again ... Take my advice, pack your bags and leave. Let the unlovable cook their own dinners, wash and iron their own clothes and stew alone in their goulash of bile and spleen.

9

Time, Space and Manners

'Good breeding differs, if at all, from high breeding
only as it gracefully remembers the rights of others,
rather than insisting on its own rights.'

Thomas Carlyle, *Sartor Resartus*

In the late spring of 1982, the *New York Times* published an
article by Mr Ron Alexander called 'Once Again, Etiquette is
a Popular Topic'. As proof of this trend he enumerated the
books that had recently been issued or were soon to be
published. Mrs Vanderbilt's book on social rituals had just
been revised by a Miss Baldridge. (This lady's name is Letitia:
she *had* to write about etiquette.) A Mrs (Mary Susan) Miller
was working with the grand-daughter of Mrs Post to bring up
to date that great lady's work on the same topic. *Miss
Manner's Guide to Excrutiatingly Correct Behaviour* by Mrs
(Judith) Martin was published in June 1982[*] and went on to
become one of the biggest bestsellers of the season. Actually,
one of the best books on the subject, *Class Acts* by Canadian
writer Eve Drobot, was published by Van Nostrand Reinhold
in that midsummer as well. Women write nearly all of the
books on this subject. There are two exceptions: *The New
Office Etiquette* by Mr George Mazzei, which concentrates
on the 'new etiquette toward women in business' and *Modern
Manners* by Mr P. J. O'Rourke, who describes himself as a
child of the sixties and who therefore has had to learn about
manners as one would a dead language – from archaeologists
of more polite periods of human history. Mr O'Rourke
apparently discovered good manners on the road to Damascus
and has been preaching the gospel ever since to the heathen
readers of *Playboy* and *Rolling Stone*.

This sudden resurgence of interest in refinement, according

[*] Atheneum, New York; Hamish Hamilton, London, 1983.

to the *New York Times'* article, was said by Mrs Mary Daly, who organizes adult-education classes in 'Style, Manners and Grace' for the Network for Learning, to have become as widespread as the desire to understand herpes. Her explanation was that Americans were scared by rising unemployment and the economic crunch. They had had a free and easy lifestyle which didn't really work and now they were clamouring for security. I doubt this exegesis. The stratum of society which is most interested in etiquette – old or new – is largely unaware that unemployment is increasing, and in any case, there is no security in etiquette. Once you know that such a thing exists, you never have another moment's peace. Life becomes as frightening and full of subtle acrimony as a game of bridge, a pastime in which the conventions change hourly for no other reason than to make the unwary players feel uncomfortable.

In the same article, Mrs Luce is quoted as saying that manners incline you to treat people with a certain distance and formality – until a friendship is formed. I, conversely, feel that as distance decreases, affection fades. One should never allow one's mind to develop poor posture through the slouch of informality. There is nothing to be gained (but much can be lost) by getting to know someone too well.

Elsewhere in the article, a Mrs (Art) Buchwald declares that the way people *look* has a lot to do with the way they *behave*. I'm sure this is true. All actors tell you that they are greatly aided in playing a part by putting on a costume for it. It would be possible to bring formal manners back to the world in an hour if a way could be discovered of gumming long white gloves on to the needle-pitted arms of teenagers.

Unfortunately this theory, though appealing in its sprightliness, would reduce courtesy to a fad. Originally politeness expressed some genuine awareness of the susceptibilities of others. This second time round it will be a passing craze and no more. If girls take to wearing ball gowns, it will be at the whim of manufacturers who wish to use up more fabric; if boys start to address their dates as 'Ma'am' and tipping their Boy George hats, it will be a joke started by a fashion magazine editor or a film director. An altered state of consciousness – a *genuine* humility – will not return. Once the arrogant idea that anyone has 'rights' has been implanted in his brain it would take neurosurgery to remove it. As Mrs Buchwald points out, 'When students lock up the dean of their college, they can't be expected to care where the glasses should go on the dinner table.' The young have always rebelled, but in earlier and simpler times, they did so laughingly. The smile of youth has now turned into a snarl. High spirits have given way to bloody-mindedness. This does not constitute an improvement.

Nevertheless, though hardly a day passes without some outrage being perpetrated in public – often in the name of political redress – books on manners continue to be written, and, at least once a month, to be borrowed by unknown readers from public libraries many years after their first publication.

In England, the eagerness to read these works does not arise from a desire to put *any*body at his ease; it is the result of a wish to save face. Sometimes it conceals an even baser motive – a longing to enter a higher society than that occupied by the climber's parents. It is thought by some that carefully mastered etiquette will render it possible to make the transition without a trace of humble origins being visible to new-found friends.

In America, the interest in guides to 'good behaviour' stems from a more altruistic motive. Hospitality is a rule in America. It is very important to Americans – a part of the way they see themselves as rich and generous Uncles. So when Americans read books about manners they are, by and large, trying to improve their hospitality.

There is a confusion in both countries about the difference between 'etiquette' and 'manners', the two terms are often used interchangeably. But etiquette is concerned with rules, its true relative is theology, not manners. Books on etiquette require hundreds of pages to list all the Dos and Don'ts as interpreted by the author from the Dead Sea Scrolls of earlier tomes and times. Books on etiquette tell you what to wear at funerals, and where to seat people at dinner parties. The advice given tends to be gravely conservative. Dinner parties are organized in strict accordance with the Noah's Ark principle: all guests are invited in male and female couples ('male and female createth He them,') or else 'paired up' by a match-making hostess, and seated in an exact arrangement as though sex were going to take place the moment the meal is over.

So marked is this principle that – if you follow the instructions – you may be required to invite guests whom you do not like simply because they are the right sex and will add 'the right touch' in these arrangements.

Even today some arbiters of etiquette such as Letitia Baldridge (in the 'Completely Revised and Updated' edition of *Amy Vanderbilt's Everyday Etiquette**) state categorically that the proper seating arrangement at a dinner party is as follows: 'The male guest of honour sits on the hostess's right, the next-most-important sits on her left. The female guest of honour sits on the host's right, and the second-most-important on his left, and so on. Husbands and wives should not be seated together.'

Mrs Judith Martin in *Miss Manners' Guide to Excrutiatingly Correct Behaviour* opts for a much more relaxed approach: 'Perhaps it is time for the givers of dinner parties to weigh the pleasures of a symmetrical table against the pleasures of being hospitable. Miss Manners, who is by no means immune to the joy of a well-ordered table, nevertheless votes for hospitality ... simply arrange your guests around the table in terms of compatibility, rather than sex ...' This cheerful bit of liberality does not extend to formal occasions, however, where Miss Manners reverts back to being 'excrutiatingly correct'.

It is not my intention to quarrel with other writers in the field. Indeed some issues of *The Times' Literary Supplement* or *The New York Review of Books* have already been so venomous that I have had to make a mad dash to the medicine cabinet for some becoming antidote. I do feel obliged to point out, however, that most books on manners are as basically conservative as Papal Encyclicals and make concessions to social change begrudgingly as if there was something wrong with life evolving to any state beyond the Middle Ages. My approach is to employ the guidelines of the past where they are still useful – otherwise I toss them aside. I believe the human mind is better engaged through imagina-

* Doubleday, 1978.

tion than obedience.

When dealing with the possibility of dinner-table embarrassments, such as those posed by today's odd couples – interracial, inter-generational, or just plain unisexual – who frequently turn out to be perfectly decent folk with a weakness for vice, one of the best ways of diplomatically concealing who is cohabiting with whom is to abandon the sit-down dinner party altogether and serve a buffet dinner party. Then the guests can mingle in an informal way and your mother-in-law need not know that your son has brought his boyfriend, or your daughter is having an affair with one of her college professors who has just left his wife and two children on her behalf. As a general rule, at any dinner party where you may sit where you like, you may assume you can sleep with whom you like.

There are many young people today who think that it is 'stuffy' and 'old fashioned' to have any rules of behaviour. Part of their attitude seems to be a legacy from the unstructured sixties when 'letting it all hang out' and 'doing your own thing' became the prevailing precepts of social behaviour for the young – with many a messy result. Another part seems to be the legacy of modern psychology from the 1920s and 1930s when parents were encouraged to be less 'repressive' and more 'permissive' in raising their children. In some families, manners went out of the window and haven't been seen since.

A rebellion against 'too much starch' in social behaviour is understandable, but a rebellion against being considerate to others is not: such a policy will surely return to haunt one – for if you are free to be inconsiderate to others, they will certainly feel free to be inconsiderate in return, and the quality of life declines steadily. I encourage people to become *conscious* of their words and actions as a means of pollution control in social relations.

Some people in contemplating my life conclude that I am much too meek and mild to set any sort of example for them – robust beings that they are, full of caffeine and nervous energy. 'You've allowed yourself to be walked over, I'm not putting up with that,' they will say, or more commonly not say but quietly think. They do not grasp that it would have been fatal for me to try to combine flamboyant strangeness with acts of hostility. I survived through politeness. What I accomplished on a small stage using the art of manners, men such as Martin Luther King and Mahatma Gandhi achieved on a much larger stage and scale. It was the genius of Gandhi to combine a philosophy of good manners with a flair for worldwide publicity. He was one part other-worldly holy man and two parts press agent. His *apparent* modesty and *apparent* humility combined with a shrewd wiliness enabled him to exploit practically any unpleasant social situation under British rule in India to his advantage. Gandhi was among the first world leaders to realize that many political acts – of brutal repression, torture and murder – are tolerated by the general public as long as its members aren't made forcibly aware of them while they are happening (the nightly coverage of the Vietnam War posed a similar obstacle to the United States government). When people were obliged to read newspaper stories or see newsreel coverage depicting a mild-mannered Indian and his followers being badly treated by the British, a climate of world opinion was created that eventually doomed any possibility of the continuation of British rule in India. Manners won.

This same technique worked in my life as well, though unlike Gandhi I did not plan any of it. When I was beaten up by bullies in the backstreets of London no one cared. People vaguely knew that such things happened but they were insulated from the details. Many years later, when the television version of *The Naked Civil Servant* was shown, however, people were moved to contemplate the indignities that I had been subjected to, and *why*, and by *whom*, and in the court of public opinion, I was not only vindicated, which was gratifying, but venerated, which was sheer ecstasy. If I were to live my life over I wouldn't go anywhere without a portable video camera.

I do not know why it is so, but there seems to be a great difference between the extent and kinds of cruelty which the public will tolerate. If cruelty is presented abstractly – a verbal report of a massacre that occurred a year ago in a country thousands of miles away – it is tolerable, but if it is presented with concrete immediacy – a film report of people being seized and tortured this very day in any part of the globe – it is not. But I suggest that this difference in tolerance for violence is one that all of us who seek a well-mannered world should exploit. Publicize all villainies, place all human evil in a limelight so that it can be seen for what it is – and not glorified as something in the 'national interest'. Maybe we should create a new sport called Bullyball in which the world's most aggressive creatures can batter themselves to smithereens and leave the rest of us alone. Mankind is in danger of being exterminated by its weakest link – macho man, a physically strong, emotionally volatile, and intellectually limited creature who is now obsolete in evolutionary terms but who is capable of causing the death of all of us through his paranoid plots. He cannot be out-gunned, out-bombed, out-missiled – he can only be outwitted. The politics of manners go far beyond the realms of behaviour mapped by Emily Post or Amy Vanderbilt. There is much more at stake here than whether one should pour tea from left to right, or right to left.

Let us consider some of these deeper implications of good manners.

All systems of *prescriptive* behaviour – morals, ethics, protocol, manners – may be said to be the imposition of form upon a dynamic reality. For a time – it may be centuries long or decades short – a near-match may occur between the mental construct and the natural world, and then, for a time, all is well – or so it seems to those who invented or represent a certain school of human behaviour. Inevitably, however, new generations, changed circumstances and 'advances in technology' alter the human reality which the system of prescriptive behaviour seeks to regulate. A gap occurs – between the new conditions of life, and the picture of how it used to be that is retained in the minds of older people. Or young people rewrite the rules. In either case, as Walter Lippmann pointed out in a famous essay, *The World Outside and the Pictures Inside Our Heads*, 'the map does not fit the territory' – small wonder that people get confused and lost. Some curse the old maps, some curse the new territory.

When a system of prescriptive behaviour does not change – indeed in some cases makes intransigence a virtue – it becomes increasingly anachronistic and even a dangerous nuisance. This process frequently makes the upholders and true believers in an old system (say, the British system of etiquette) even more dedicated to maintaining its traditions. The problem with most old systems of behaviour is not that they are old nor even that they resist change, but that their High Priests and followers develop a siege-mentality and end up being *opposed* to change, pitting the past against the present in yet another needless struggle.

In order to survive, systems of prescriptive behaviour must adapt; the spirit of a code must always be seen as more important than the letter of its laws. Failure to change, when change is due, only undermines respect for the entire system. If one associates 'morality' with some puritanical person or some zealous organization which is *against* practically everything one is not going to have much use for 'moral principles'. If one associates 'manners' with some sort of dainty matriarchal dictatorship, then one is going to be tempted to ignore the whole business as pre-feminist silliness.

In the 1980s, any man who, on principle, escorts a woman down the city streets by walking on the outside – originally conceived as a courtesy to protect M'lady from the hazards of horse-drawn carriages – now exposes her to the more likely discomfort of being dripped on by air conditioners or shat upon by pigeons. This is only a small example of the calamities that may occur by maintaining an abstract rule that once made sense. Just as there are 'dead languages' and 'living languages' so too are there 'dead manners' and 'living manners'. While the dead manners of the past may be of interest to archivists and historians, they must never be mistaken for the more sensible designs for living which are, closer to the needs of contemporary people.

We often hear that there has been a 'decline in manners' – but what does this mean? If we were to cite one hundred rules of etiquette that prevailed a century ago and now found that eighty-seven of them are no longer observed (except at weddings and funerals, where perhaps 50 per cent are still in effect), we would not prove that manners have declined, only that certain quaint customs have gone. For manners to truly decline there must be a measurable diminution in the impulse to be mannerly, or a lack of knowledge of what mannerly behaviour consists of now, coupled with a lack of interest in acquiring such knowledge. There is no proof of this: wherever I have travelled in the United States I have found an avid interest in the subject. Manners are an art of living and, like any other art, they undergo changes in appearance, even in substance, and certainly in style, though the impulse which creates them remains constant in every age. Howling about manners declining is rather like calling Picasso a bad artist because he doesn't paint like Rembrandt. As modern people we have the duty to reappraise everything so that the art, science, law, religion and manners of our century reflect the best of our current knowledge and our most enlightened thinking.

Confusion about how to behave in certain situations contributes to gaffes: does a man open every door for a woman, or in these days of claimed equality with the scales having fallen from their eyes do they take turns? This is a problem fairly easily solved: I would say that whoever is best able to open the door, depending on what kind of door it is, should gracefully contrive to reach it first and that the sex of this person is immaterial. There are, however, more complex factors in contemporary mass society that appear to predispose people to rudeness – not the least of which is the strain on the psyche and the nervous system of living in noisy, polluted, overcrowded places.

In one of the best analyses of our present social condition – *Human Scale* by Kirkpatrick Sale* – the author contends that:

A person surrounded by subways and blaring radios, beset on every side with clamour, confusion, filth, boredom and hopelessness, might well strike out in rage when provoked; a person surrounded by calm decorousness, purposefulness and comfort is less likely to. Behaviour basically depends on the setting, the time and place and society in which it occurs. Obviously the desired goal is to find those settings in which the benevolent side of our human nature is encouraged and the malevolent side dampened. That will not ensure constant and unvarying social harmony, it seems safe to say, but it certainly will go a long way to permitting it and fostering it.

* Coward, McCann, 1981.

There is a debate among sociologists now about whether it is crowded living conditions, higher densities, sheer numbers or the amount of interaction that produces the individual and collective pathologies of big cities. Biological studies show almost uniformly that crowding and high densities in animal populations produce such things as hypertension, stress, aggression, violence, exhaustion, sadism, mental disorder, infertility, disease, suicide and death. For the human animal, rather more adaptable to its surroundings, the evidence is not quite so unequivocal, but ever since the work of Mr Georg Simmel at the turn of the century it has been fairly well recognized that masses of people create masses of social problems. The more people the more problems.

Bad manners may be seen as a distant early warning of more serious social problems in gestation. With more people there are bound to be more contacts among them on any given day. The New York Regional Plan Association has determined that there are 11,000 people within a ten-minute radius in Nassau County, 20,000 in Newark, New Jersey, and 220,000 in Manhattan – and so to prevent a psychosocial 'overload' a city dweller must either have fewer contacts, spend less time on any single contact, or be less intense and involved during any contact. That's what produces the familiar pattern of contemporary big cities. People create fewer contacts by developing ethnic ties and consequent separation from 'outside' groups. They have unlisted telephone numbers, don't make eye contact with people on the street, and ignore lifelong neighbours. They spend less time per contact by cutting out traditional courtesies such as 'sorry' and 'please', by treating supermarket checkers and short-order waitresses as faceless and history-less and by refusing 'to get involved'. And they reduce the intensity of each contact by limiting their 'span of sympathy' (in sociological parlance) to the immediate family, by supporting governmental agencies that take over their personal commitments (welfare, for example) and by emphasizing their privacy through personal-space 'cocoons' in a lift or café – the *I'm-All-Right, Jack* Walkman crowd.

A number of scholarly studies have compared the civilities of people in large cities with those in smaller places, and with rare uniformity they show big-city dwellers to be, as the stereotypes would indicate, far more selfish, hostile to strangers, unhelpful and unfriendly. In one study, a group of researchers dialled phone numbers at random in various-sized cities and, concocting a plausible story about an emergency, asked the people who answered to look up and call a number for them and leave a vital message; people in the smaller cities were far more responsive. In another study, stamped envelopes were casually left around at restaurants, and the like in different-sized cities. The ones from the smaller places were mailed back much more often. Students at the City University of New York compared the responses of people in Manhattan with those in small cities in upstate Rockland County when asked by strangers if they could come in and use the phone; an average of 27 per cent of the New Yorkers allowed people in, compared to 72 per cent of the others. And one researcher placed abandoned cars in middle-class neighbourhoods, first near New York University in a city of seven million and then near Stanford University in a city of nearly 20,000, and discovered that the car in New York was rapidly stripped and gutted while the one in Stanford was actually guarded by passers-by against attempts to damage it. What is interesting about all of these examples is that the very qualities of civility that the urban setting has traditionally been supposed to foster – the word 'civility', after all, comes from the Latin for city – are least in evidence there.

This doesn't mean that anyone interested in a mannerly life should abandon London for Leeds, or New York for Eugene, Oregon. It is certainly possible, as Jane Jacobs has documented in her classic book, *The Life and Death of American Cities*, to preserve an active sense of community within a district of a large city that is *not* based on xenophobia (establishing a ghetto for people of only one kind), through the formation of Block Associations and other conscious and deliberate efforts of good neighbourliness. By understanding how a particular environment has a destructive effect upon social relations, one can devise strategies to mitigate the damage, and even, in some cases, prevent it from occurring.

Crisp's last law: *Reading books on manners and appreciating what good behaviour is in all aspects of one's personal and social life is not enough; if one is constantly frustrated and defeated by the environment in which one lives good manners will remain an elusive, abstract goal rather than an embodied idea.* We must at all times seek out those people and situations most conducive to bringing out the best in us, and keep to a minimum our contacts with people who merely drain our energy.

It is my view that the British system of etiquette – which is a class system based on snobbery and exclusion – is in its last-gasp stage, and that the American revolution in manners – creating a humanistic base for hospitality based on a principle of kindness and inclusion – will prevail in the future. I believe that we have to recognize that modern societies are changing quickly and that no inflexible and hidebound system of behaviour is capable of providing people with useful 'maps' to the social landscapes that are evolving all around us. The British system, which aspires to find a place for everything and keep everything in its place, will not serve as a guide to the future.

In America practically everyone regards himself as middle class and is proud of it, whereas in England to call something 'middle class' is to condemn it. (Having pottery ducks on your walls would stamp you as indisputably lower middle class in England, but in America the harshest comment that would be made about having such ducks on your walls is that you must be into 'fifties kitsch'. Things are dated by time here and to some extent by taste but never by class.)

There is a mad desire to be fashionable in America, to change when things change and always in order to seem young. There is much less desire to seem young in England, but in America youth is not merely a phase through which one passes but a lifelong value. There may be seven ages of man, according to Shakespeare, but in America there is only one that matters – perpetual adolescence. On the other hand, Americans, unlike the English, show little interest in seeming aristocratic or refined, although there are the occasional jokes about people who came over on the *Mayflower*. Debrett has now produced a book called *The Texan Aristocracy*, but this is a misnomer because it's really about the rich, and while great wealth may create a glassy shield around certain

Americans it does not bestow any of the attributes of aristocracy.

When Americans parade their wealth, they do so chiefly in the form of extreme generosity. When I visited Texas, during my lecture tour, I found this to be overwhelming. I was practically handed the keys to the cities of Austin and Houston, but not having been raised with my own Neiman-Marcus charge account, I had no idea what to do with such extravagant gifts. The American habit of generosity includes the desire to make others feel at home and to make everyone feel that they are your equal, though not perhaps in wealth. Some years ago in Los Angeles I attended an awards ceremony, the star of which was Miss Julie Harris. There was a moment when I asked my companion if Miss Harris had arrived. He stood up and looked about, and then seeing her on the far side of the room, walked over to where she was, evidently to ask her if there was a moment when I might be presented to her. She immediately got up from her table, left everything, and crossed the room in order to present herself to me. This is an instance of the way that the American idea of generosity, hospitality and good manners work. They endeavour to always make the first move, and they are concerned about creating the impression that it is an honour for *them* to meet *you*.

When people say that Americans are rude they usually mean that they are nosy, and they are, they long to know everything about you and they quite unabashedly *ask* everything about you, in the middle of the street, even in the dead of winter, but this is because they feel they are your friends, so they don't see their curiosity about you as an invasion of privacy.

The English believe people wish to preserve their privacy and that this should not be invaded by total strangers, particularly not at awkward times. The basic distinction between the two attitudes is whether you treasure more the whole world or your own privacy. I myself do not want any privacy and am pleased to talk to anybody including total strangers about any aspect of my life. All that I ask is that I be left completely alone for one or two days of the week to recover from the ravages of my sociability.

Although there is a reverence for the young in America, there is no blame laid upon people simply because they are old, an attitude which exists in England, where anyone who is having a jolly life at the age of sixty is treated with derision. People keep telling you how ancient you are; they are almost asking, why don't you just lie down and die?

In America, people like Katharine Hepburn, Helen Hayes, Ruth Gordon, to name a few of the actresses who keep on working come hell or arthritis, are regarded practically as heroic figures. In England, the old tend to be pushed aside as dotty relics; but in America, if you can run around Central Park at the age of eighty-six someone is bound to put you on television – on a cable TV show at least, for the deregulated airwaves are an arid waste in constant need of irrigation. Contra Mr Orwell: in America people are grateful that they are *worth* watching.

In sum: *if manners present a particular difficulty in England it is how to leave people their privacy without seeming to shun them, and in America the difficulty is how to offer people your friendship without seeming to intrude.* The American way of manners appeals to me, suits me: I am free to go about in an open society. In New York, where everyone who is not hitting you over the head is your lifelong friend, I have grown accustomed to the paradoxical pleasures of American life. Here in the land of fifty million handguns there is greater interest in, and greater potential for, creating a civilized, humanistic society, open to all and barring none, than anywhere else on earth. In Russia, or Cuba, the likes of me would long ago have been liquidated. In Chile I would disappear, in Israel I would be ostracized, in Iran I would be shot, in England I would have – as I did have – a punishing work record and a meagre pension. Only in America am I encouraged to *enjoy* every aspect of a personal renascence, instead of accepting an enforced senescence, upon reaching my golden age.

Once, when my mother was telling me about her school-days, she said, 'I never liked mathematics, there was only one right answer.' So I think she *would* have liked the American way of manners, for there there are many answers to all social problems, and the only thing that matters is that one's behaviour is motivated by a consideration for others. It is enough to be approximately correct in one's social behaviour. America alone, among the countries I am familiar with, has the flexibility to change, to incorporate change, and to keep addressing the future on terms that are relevant and self-correcting. Even Americans, of course, are sometimes caught napping (as we have seen in recent years in the automotive and computer industries, where Japan leapt to the lead) but, unlike England, there is nothing inherently resistant to change in the social infrastructure. On the everyday level, this means that Americans are more capable than the English of creating a truly hospitable society in which everyone is treated as an equal, without having to overcome the deeply rooted prejudices of a class system *in addition* to having to overcome prejudices concerning race, religion, sex and nationality. In short, Americans have one less handicap to overcome than the English in creating a future society in which a majority of its citizens feel that they are accepted and welcomed.

The difference may seem minor and inconclusive – but when one is living through an epidemic of rudeness one has to call upon whatever medical supplies are available. In that sense I hail America as the country best able to create a healthy climate for modern manners and to replace outmoded forms of etiquette which only hurt or hinder people in being misapplied past their expiry date.

IO

Designs for Living

> 'Everything that can be thought at all can be thought clearly. Everything that can be said can be said clearly.'
>
> Ludwig Wittgenstein, *Tractatus Logico-Philosophicus*

If I were to live my life over again, even though I have committed no crime that deserves the punishment of reincarnation, I would create a new profession: Manners Consultant. Such an occupation would suit me well; I could just *be* – and talk. I would offer my advice to engineers and architects so that when they build a new airliner or design a new shopping plaza it would be built in a way that is conducive to good manners by its future users rather than being a hindrance to politeness, as one so often finds in the social planning that exists today. It is an old maxim that 'man shapes his buildings and then his buildings shape him'. I will now consider the ways in which good behaviour can be encouraged in people through better industrial and social design.

For example: the Second Avenue bus I am riding on is in most respects an adequate vehicle but it has not been designed with good manners in mind. It has plenty of window space but the glass is tinted to a shade of such duskiness that the passengers have difficulty in keeping their bearings en route and spend a lot of time poking past their neighbours and peering through the purple haze to see if they are nearing their stop. The mechanical engineer who chose this shade of glass presumably figured he was doing passengers a favour in shielding them from the occasional ray of the sun, though it would be more polite to permit each passenger to decide for himself if and when he wants solar protection, and then to wear his sunglasses. Perhaps the engineer is a fan of Mr Eliot who once spoke of going out 'into the violet hour' or perhaps his mother sang *Deep Purple* to him as a child – whatever the reasons for all this mandatory mauve the result is irritation for just about everybody, and serious inconvenience to anyone whose vision is impaired.

Tinted glass is not the bus's only design flaw. The windows are constructed in such a way that only a few inches of ventilation are allowed by sliding the front portion of the window to the back or the rear portion to the front, but the openings do not correspond to any of those seats midway between these long windows. This means that at least one third of the passengers (on a full busload) do not have the option of having a breeze. Compounding what is already an inconsiderate design, the windows if opened direct a blast of air against the person sitting next to the opening, while the person who *wants* fresh air receives barely a rumour of the ill wind that is blowing him no good. He can tell there is a funnelled gust of air coming in by the way in which the hair (let's hope it's not a vulnerable hairpiece) of the person sitting in front is flying and flapping in all directions. As a result of this design, most people seated next to a window keep it closed and want it closed, while the people directly in front and behind are reduced to sweltering in an atmosphere of oppressive humidity and body odours.

To make matters even worse, the heating and air-conditioning system of the bus has its eccentricities. Either it doesn't work so that in winter everyone is shivering or else it overworks, won't stop and everyone is sweating. In three years of living in New York I have not been lucky enough to find more than the odd bus in which the air-conditioning system was working properly – and as many buses are hermetically sealed and one cannot open *any* of the windows (some engineer thought *that* would be a good idea) the failure of an air-conditioning system is critical when the temperature soars.

None of these irritations are necessary but they exist because the people responsible for social planning forgot to put the 'manners programme' into their computers when their designs were embryonic.

These particular failures may not apply to public transportation in every city, but each city has its own peculiar civic hiccups which contribute to an erosion of manners. In London the doubledecker buses help to prevent the intense overcrowding that one finds on New York buses during rush hours – but many of the routes of the London buses are incomprehensible unless you have lived twenty years in the city, whereas in New York there is a map, easy to follow, posted thoughtfully at practically every bus stop outlining where you are and where the bus at that stop will be going. In no time one can master the routes, though traffic is often so congested it may take several days to get across town.

The subways that are offered for the safety of pedestrians and the efficiency of moving traffic in London, alleviate potential for the kind of hit-and-miss pile-ups of cars and people that occur at practically every New York intersection, but many of the subways require a person to climb up and down a lot of steep steps and this is hardly a pleasure for those with any of a number of health problems. In certain other cities such as Montreal, and Toronto, the subways are not only quiet, and impeccably clean, but (with considerate planning) offer escalators as well as stairs to the public, so that no one need emerge from the underground looking like a miner at day's end in a Newcastle pit.

So far I have only mentioned certain modes of public transportation and their defects – the day is only beginning. Everywhere we go in the city – the bank, the post office, the supermarket and so on – we meet with defects in design that undermine our manners. I could say – I *do* say – that no matter what happens to one in the course of a day one should try to be forbearing and to wait until you get home to have a good cry. The people in charge of the aesthetic layout of a bank or a department store or a government office have the power to help make our transactions go smoothly and pleasantly, so that our good manners would be given encouragement. Perhaps even more importantly the *policies* of banks, stores and government offices should aim to be as clear, efficient and polite as possible; no one should be made to feel that he is wasting his own or anyone else's time.

Many new stores and offices are constructed with 'efficiency', 'economy' and 'safety' in mind but these considerations –

particularly the corners that are cut in the name of 'economy' – are insufficient to construct a comfortable environment which elicits the best possible behaviour from people. If one builds an environment for human beings which carelessly adds one frustration to another, then no matter how majestic it looks, or how astronomical the cost, those human beings will resent it, hate it, deface it and some may even try to destroy it. Designers of buildings and products alike should seek to reduce the social alienation that already exists in most cities by learning more about people as they really are and applying this knowledge to their architecture and their manufacturing.

Given, however, that it is often a struggle to get designers to put 'safety first' (we are all familiar with hearing about fires causing more deaths than they might have done due to toxic fumes from plastic materials that should never have been used but which were cheap), I do not hold out much hope that the concept of promoting good manners through enlightened engineering will sweep through the boardrooms of McDonnell Douglas, Ford and Mitsubishi in the near future. Rather, like any idea slightly ahead of its time, the burden of its survival falls upon a few concerned individuals.

One way of minimizing the pressures of an average day in a big city is to counter-programme one's activities (in the parlance of televisionaries) so that when 60 per cent of the population is making a mad dash to the tube you go shopping instead; and when hordes of whey-faced city-dwellers descend upon Hampstead Heath you stroll round Soho. There is, admittedly, a problem with this theory of crowd-avoidance once a city reaches the proportions of a megapolis such as Tokyo, London or New York, for then you will find thousands of people milling about at every hour of the day and will only have the choice between bad and worse. Still, it is a means of reducing slightly the strain upon one's nervous system and hence one's manners.

Another way in which the individual can improve his manners is by deliberately slowing down. The busier you are the more your manners will decline, and then you will excuse yourself by saying that you haven't got time for Crispian flourishes and that people will just have to understand if you take short cuts in courtesy. 'I have no time for all this bowing and scraping,' you will say to yourself with an ego as big as Texas, 'people will just have to get used to me the way I am.' This will not do. We are all horrible the way we are, and no one should be asked to put up with our *natural* selves or see us as we really are, ever.

We must live a life where we *do* have the time for others. We must reduce our activities so that we are never living at the very edge of our nervous or physical energy; then we will always have the time to behave nicely. There is no excuse for always being late, for always being on the run, for foolishly allowing yourself to get *desperate* over anything. It is better to be a polite invalid than someone who enjoys rude health.

All situations can be dealt with more successfully with what is called tact and forbearance. The less you get in the habit of expressing irritation the less you will feel. It is quite untrue that one should 'get rid of one's aggressions' – give way, throw a chair out the window, curse and swear at the least provocation – it only adds to your rage. The same is true of depression. If you go around feeling that no one has ever been as miserable as you, and that you can't be expected to be considerate when you're so miserable, you will not behave well towards others – and neither will they behave well towards you. All you have done is create a pretext for behaving badly. Depression, like most emotions, should be suppressed and endured privately. Show me someone who advocates shameless self-expression and I'll show you someone with a whim of iron.

We live now in a world where protest is virtually unnecessary, but what is so extraordinary is that there are more strikes, more marches and demonstrations in the world than ever before. None at all are needed, for people today have far more latitude in their choices than existed when I was young. When I was a teenager *everything* that a person did was liable to be criticized and there was no worse offence than being unlike other people. Nowadays this regimental attitude has completely disappeared. A girl may look like a boy trying to look like a girl who is trying to look like a boy – and no one cares. There are public orgies down at the docks – and no one cares. No man is penalized for wearing make-up any more. The habit of indulgent self-expression, as I have rueful cause to know, only leads a person to require ever larger amounts of public attention.

Far from encouraging what is most monstrous in us to grow ever larger and stronger – our impatience, our bad temper – we should be concerned with bringing what is most savage in us under control.

There are various ways in which you can indicate to people that, although you really like their company, you have your own life to lead and that they must fit in with it. It is up to you to set the guidelines, so that people will not take advantage of you – and so that you will be relieved of the temptation to speak badly of them as soon as they leave the room. It is up to you to let people know, early and clearly, what your limits are, for in the present era of great personal freedom it's more difficult for anyone to decide what are good manners and what aren't. It is not up to me to lay down absolute rules, and it is not up to others to guess what your limits may be; it is up to you to avoid ambiguities in the troublesome areas – such as sex, money and self-esteem – where there are considerable differences in tolerances and taste and where, without a clear signal from you, those with whom you socialize are likely to make mistakes.

The good habit of being clear will, with some practice, become as much a part of one's 'second nature' as the bad habit of being scatterbrained was in the past. But it must be cultivated, with conscious effort: when, for example, you are ordering some item by telephone from a newspaper advertisement or a catalogue, you should first write down what it is you wish to order, what serial number it has, your choice of colour and style if that is pertinent, and the number of your account or charge card. Then you can say, with maximum efficiency, when the sales operator answers your call, 'Good morning, I would like to order one dozen widgets, item 6718, from the hardware department, my account number is 009610 . . .' and so on. There is no excuse for being unprepared when you place a call – it isn't as if you have been caught offguard by the store calling you. Even when you ring up a friend I would recommend having pen and paper handy, in the event you are given some information that needs to be jotted down. Even apart from that exigency, you should draw up a short list of the topics you wish to discuss before placing the call so that nothing is missed, and you don't waste anyone's time by thinking aloud or trying to remember if there was anything else you wanted to say. You should think *before* you speak and it wouldn't hurt to write out a few lines of what you intend to say, so that you develop the habit of speaking concisely and politely but nevertheless getting to the point.

Some people have no idea how often they say 'you know ...' or 'you see ...' or 'well, hmmm', and while putting a lot of dead time in their conversation is not technically a breach of manners, it is nevertheless a bad habit and an impediment to smooth social relations.

Clear communication is the most important tool of good manners, and anything that can be done to make one more conscious of what one is saying and how one is saying it is likely to improve all of one's social relations. I have no use for swear words as a form of emphasis. I feel, perhaps erroneously, that I can convey my anger without dragging my genitals into the conversation, or the gruesome details of physical processes. I suppose if you can be *sure* that your audience will in no way be offended you can say anything you please, but you have to judge the suitability of what you are about to say by the standards of the weakest member of your audience, so that if someone of sixty is present your anecdotes will be more discreet, I would think, than if only hot-blooded teenagers are present. And at the other end of the age scale, if someone who is only twelve is present, and he or she is not already a junkie or child-prostitute, you restrain your remarks accordingly. The more mixed the company in age, sex, class and nationality, the more uncertain you will be about what their view of morality is and the less free you will be to use words or say things that may give offence.

At one time you could never say anything that referred to your sexual activities at all; nowadays a woman may tell you she has the curse and a man may tell you about his piles. While this is hailed in some quarters as a breakthrough I fail to see how it advances the art of conversation. When I was young I remember reading Lady George's *Book of Etiquette* which made all sorts of strict stipulations for a morally squeaky-clean life, such as: 'The setting up of books by male authors next to books by females is absolutely forbidden.' Now the pendulum of what-is-proper has swung so far the other way that it is not uncommon to be greeted by a most gracious hostess, who surrounds herself with all the accoutrements of *The New Yorker* lifestyle, with the words, 'You know, what I need is a good f**k.' When people say things like that they do so to show that they *can* – although there are at least ten better ways of conveying their meaning. They do not intend necessarily to offend, shock or titillate, but to express an image they have of themselves as *totally* free, uninhibited bohemians. These Anglo-Saxon oinks and grunts are the verbal equivalent of wearing gaudy clothes. It's amazing how vain some people are over what they look like, but how vacant they are about what they *sound* like.

People are more likely to forgive you for uttering expletives under stress than for decorating an ordinary conversation with obscenities. A steady diet of the shortest-words-for-the-longest-things is never a good idea for you *may* give offence, which is bad manners, and you will certainly make your conversation monotonous, which is bad style. A lot of people know perhaps five thousand words and only use about two thousand of them in their entire conversation. They feel somewhat at a loss to say how *amazing* something was, how *annoying* something was, how *terrifying*, how *wonderful*, so they include words which they feel add something but which in fact add nothing. Whenever I hear the word 'f**k', I hear it often not so much applied to sex but, preposterously, to such things as traffic lights that have turned red, vending units that won't work, pay telephones that won't telephone or pay. This usually strikes me as an impoverishment of language. It is hard to say what is being insulted more – sexual functions or mechanical dysfunctions – but what comes across even more clearly is that the person is not really connecting well within his own brain. His language has taken on a ruttish life of its own, it is no longer the flexible tool of a reflective mind.

One of the reasons why people talk and behave in an ill-mannered fashion is that at the age of sixteen or seventeen they got into the defiance-racket and never got out. This usually happens because they were taught manners (along with everything else) by a rudely authoritarian teacher (of the 'Do as I say not as I do' variety); the kind who unconsciously incites his students to lifelong rebellion. I can remember when I was at school that we boys often felt that we were being made fun of by teachers who seized every opportunity to humiliate us. Our tone of voice was mimicked. The teacher would say, '*Please*, sir, what is it?' in a whiney voice of gross exaggeration. This was quite unnecessary, and we grew up to be rude and ruined, warped and defiant. What children need is not bland praise, but astute guidance in a form that doesn't make them feel inadequate.

I have known teachers who, when a student hands in a piece of, say, artwork and says, 'It still isn't right, I'm afraid,' pounce immediately with the full force of their authority and reply, 'No, it isn't right for the simple reason that you haven't done what I told you to do.' It would be much better for the teacher to say, 'Perhaps I didn't make myself quite clear, you must look at the sky more carefully. Now do you really think it's the same shade of blue from end to end?' And when the tiny student of tiny talent says, 'Yes,' the teacher may point out, 'Doesn't that bit on the horizon seem a bit paler?' The student squints and dawdles, but after a second look, says, 'Oh yes, it is a bit paler'; then the teacher says, 'I suggest you include this new observation in your work.' And then the pupil goes back and erases, and changes the drawing, and will be pleased that he is doing things better.

One should teach people things indirectly so that they seem to discover what they need to know for themselves, rather than reducing them to tears for not memorizing what they have been taught. I would never be unkind to children and I certainly wouldn't scold them. If we want the young to be well behaved it is up to us who are older to set a cheerful and benign example. Only dogs should be sent to Obedience School and that is because dogs, particularly German Shepherds, have all read *Mein Kampf* and love to follow leaders. In the rearing of children, as in any crisis, the words '... because I say so' are insulting. As with adults so with a child, it is impolite to discuss with him or even in his presence any subject for which no explanation is on offer. What young people find so detestable about their elders it not their sins but their secrets – and their smugness.

I suppose that no one knows the true meaning of ambivalence until they have had a child – or anything else small and cuddly, pukey and poopy, that is totally dependent upon one for its well-being when young but can't wait to be old enough to bite the hand that feeds it. I recommend keeping one's life as uncomplicated as possible, I don't even like to have plants around the house demanding, 'Feed me, feed me', but I recognize that most human beings feel compelled to have little carbon units to whom they can pass on their ignorance and so that the traditions of chronic poverty will not be broken.

And where will it all end?

We might even ask ourselves where will it all begin? A pregnant woman asked of Fate only that her child should be well mannered. Unbeknown to her she was carrying twins. They were never born because they stood for ever at the exit from her womb, the one saying, 'After you, Claude,' while his brother said, 'No. After you, Cecil.'

While it is *theoretically* possible to be too self-effacing, in the world in which we live our precarious lives it is unlikely that anyone will ever suffer from an excess of deferentiality. (Crisp's general rule: *If you can't beat them, join them; if you can't join them, grovel* ...) The greatest difficulty lies in deciding where kindness ends and good manners begin. We are never accused of displaying bad manners in our treatment of animals but we may be accused of unkindness. There was even a time when we could not be accused of bad manners towards our servants and before that when no one could be accused of cruelty towards a slave. Manners do not grow in mountainous country. Manners are for the plains where no one is above or below us; and indeed, the well-mannered treat all people as their equals.

When I was young the guides to good behaviour instructed readers how to behave by offering absolute rules of etiquette, although few were as extreme as the following: 'A boy should blow his nose with a handkerchief in the presence of a superior. He should not wet his tongue with his lips, should not swallow his saliva but should stamp on his spit, should not sit with his legs apart or scratch himself or clean his teeth with his knife; he should not throw gristle under the table and not feed other people's dogs when dining with them, should wipe the wine cup before passing it on. Even when undressing alone, remember that the angels dislike the exposure of private parts....' (This is actually from a text by Catherine of Aragon, which had gone through 120 editions by 1780.)

Such edicts will strike the modern reader as ridiculous. It is the fate of all guides to good manners to be laughed at eventually, particularly those that are not intentionally funny. If it may be said that this book makes a modest contribution to the literature of manners I hope it will be in the form of reversing the usual response of readers of laughing at the moral earnestness of the author – by their taking seriously what is presented lightly. Even with paradoxes there is a better or worse way for responses to run.

Remember: great stylists do not surround themselves with dullards. Good conversation stimulates better conversation; wit provokes wit. If even a small portion of the charm and grace which you cultivate in yourself rubs off on others through your transactions, the tone of society will be raised that much more and all of our lives will be enhanced.

There are in our midst nuclear nihilists who say that because mankind is threatened with extinction, nothing matters any more, anything goes, what the hell – but in fact it is all the more important for us to make an effort to climb to the highest rung of civilization that we are capable of reaching.

So every day out there in the hack-and-stab world, when you tip your hat and say something kind you have at least joined the forces of people who are trying to make life bearable and better, as opposed to those who don't give a damn and steadily make matters worse. Give us this day our daily struggle and with any luck our manners will triumph.

Quentin Crisp

How to Become
a Virgin

After fifty years of almost unalleviated obscurity Quentin Crisp found fame at last when a film based on his autobiography *The Naked Civil Servant* appeared on television throughout the world.

In this second volume of autobiography, peppered with trenchant anecdotes and polished epigrams, Quentin Crisp describes the wider horizons of his years as a celebrity at home and abroad, his own personal philosophy of inaction and his love affair with North America.

How to Become a Virgin is as wise and witty, acute and perceptive as its inimitable author.

'If Quentin Crisp had never existed it is unlikely that anyone would have had the nerve to invent him' *The Times*

'Quentin Crisp is a tonic and a delight' *Guardian*

Quentin Crisp

The Naked
Civil Servant

Quentin Crisp has been described as one of London's works of art: he has become a celebrity, through his lifestyle, through the much-acclaimed TV dramatization of *The Naked Civil Servant*, and through his one-man show.

In this moving and funny autobiography, he describes his unhappy childhood and the stresses of adolescence which led him to London. There, in bed-sitting rooms and cafés, he found a world of brutality and comedy, of short-lived jobs and precarious relationships. It was a life he faced with courage, humour and intelligence.

'Brilliant, full of sardonic humour and sharp spurts of wit' – *Irish Times*

'If Quentin Crisp had never existed it is unlikely that anyone would have had the nerve to invent him' – *The Times*

'Quentin Crisp is a tonic and a delight' – *Guardian*

FLAMINGO

FLAMINGO

Flamingo is a quality imprint publishing both fiction and non-fiction. Below are some recent titles.

Fiction
- [ ] Troubles *J. G. Farrell* £2.95
- [ ] Rumours of Rain *André Brink* £2.95
- [ ] The Murderer *Roy Heath* £1.95
- [ ] A Legacy *Sybille Bedford* £2.50
- [ ] The Old Jest *Jennifer Johnston* £1.95
- [ ] Dr Zhivago *Boris Pasternak* £3.50
- [ ] The Leopard *Giuseppe di Lampedusa* £2.50
- [ ] The Mandarins *Simone de Beauvoir* £3.95

Non-fiction
- [ ] Freud and Man's Soul *Bruno Bettelheim* £2.50
- [ ] On the Perimeter *Caroline Blackwood* £1.95
- [ ] A Journey in Ladakh *Andrew Harvey* £2.50
- [ ] The French *Theodore Zeldin* £3.95
- [ ] The Practice of History *Geoffrey Elton* £2.50
- [ ] Camera Lucida *Roland Barthes* £2.50
- [ ] Image Music Text *Roland Barthes* £2.95
- [ ] A Ragged Schooling *Robert Roberts* £2.50
- [ ] The Naked Civil Servant *Quentin Crisp* £2.50

You can buy Flamingo paperbacks at your local bookshop or newsagent. Or you can order them from Fontana Paperbacks, Cash Sales Department, Box 29, Douglas, Isle of Man. Please send a cheque, postal or money order (not currency) worth the purchase price plus 15p per book (maximum postal charge is £3.00 for orders within the UK).

NAME (Block letters) _____

ADDRESS_____

_____

_____